TRUTH IN WORDS

TRUTH IN WORDS

B Y

ANTONY SNELL
of the Society of the Sacred Mission

'The way in which assumptions excite no question, and people go on spinning arguments, as if the whole of the invisible world was as easy to be understood as the theory of the steam engine, has long been one of my standing wonders. . . . I am glad that you have brought out so strongly the two-sided character of all our means of knowing, and the fact that what we know in religious matters is but the tendency to know. The idea of perfect and absolute knowledge, which is involved in so much of what is said and taught on all sides, becomes daily more and more unendurable to me.'

(R. W. CHURCH to J. B. MOZLEY, 1855.)

THE FAITH PRESS
7 Tufton Street London SW 1

FIRST PUBLISHED IN GREAT BRITAIN

© *Antony Snell*, S.S.M., *1965*

230·03
Sn 27 t

PRINTED IN GREAT BRITAIN
in 11 point Baskerville type
BY THE FAITH PRESS LTD.
LEIGHTON BUZZARD

CONTENTS

PREFACE

THE aim of this book is to estimate the place of authoritative verbal matter in a Christian's faith. There are few subjects about which Christians differ from each other more than they do about this; and there are few about which they find it harder to give sympathetic attention to each other's point of view. To many people written texts of some kind, whether Scripture, Creeds, or ecclesiastical definitions, are almost the foundations of their faith. To others, such texts are at best helpful but rather uncertain illustrations of it.

The book is necessarily written from a definite point of view, and on definite assumptions, which are not supposed to be proved within its covers. The point of view is well illustrated in the quotation from Dean Church printed on the title page; and a main assumption about the nature and function of the Church is postulated, that it is guided by the Holy Spirit, and has the function of teaching its members in his Name.

But I hope my presentation of the argument is sufficiently free from tactless dogmatism to win a patient attention to it from people whose sympathy with the writer's point of view is quite incomplete. If I have chosen the right topics for discussion, and have discussed them rationally, this hope may be justified. For this reason the book begins with a short panorama of the argument, so as to provide a sort of rationale of it.

I am especially grateful to two members of the community to which I belong for direct help with the MS, and to many others for help of a less direct kind.

ANTONY SNELL, S.S.M.

St. Michael's House,
Crafers, South Australia

CHAPTER I

A PANORAMA OF THE SUBJECT

THE function of this chapter might to a large extent have been performed by a fairly detailed Table of Contents, and normal convention would have been more closely followed if it had been. But the subject which is to be discussed in this book raises so many questions of very wide range and generality that some kind of explanation is wanted of why just *these* questions have been chosen for discussion, why in just *this* form, and in just *this* sequence. It would be hard to devise a Table of Contents which helped at all towards such an explanation.

There is a further reason for beginning with a sort of panorama: many of the particular lines of argument are so very general, and it is often so hard to see how far they are supposed to be applicable in detail, that it should be useful to know from the beginning what place each large topic is taken to have in the whole discussion. The order in which the topics are dealt with may perhaps seem arbitrary or wrong, but it will certainly be as well to know why it has been adopted.

We are accustomed to hearing extreme things said about the place of verbal matter in our faith: both on the general question, and on the special position in it of particular verbal matter, whether Scripture, Creeds, or other ecclesiastical formulae. All these texts are certainly in some sense authoritative: what can this authority be rationally taken to be, and what should it in fact be taken to be?

The general subject may be divided into two main questions: first, what authority could verbal matter have? and secondly, what is the status in this respect of this and that kind of relevant matter? The former of these main divisions raises questions to the discussion of which the next five chapters are devoted; and the latter is discussed in two separate chapters, one for Scripture and the other for non-scriptural matter. These two chapters are numbers Seven and Eight in this book. The main line of the argument will require some discussion of heresy and schism, since the duty of willing conformity with the life of the Church is throughout taken to be the real meaning of authority in matters of belief, as also in all other matters which concern Christian faith and practice : and if in matters of belief, then plainly in what concerns the authority of such written matter as expresses such things.

What can usefully be attempted now is a short preview of the topics selected for discussion in the next five chapters, which ought to show how they connect with each other. The main questions seem to be, first, the nature, place, and scope of authority in the Christian faith, and, secondly, the possible place of written matter in relation to this authority. It is easy to see that such a review might involve almost all possible questions both of theory and of practice. This being an impossible undertaking, it remains to attempt a justification of the questions actually to be raised and discussed.

An attempt is made in the next chapter to compare and correlate the two commonly distinguished meanings of the word authority, with an eye on their application to written matter : the first of these meanings is the right to command obedience, and the second is a proper influence over opinion, justified by knowledge and competence. Both meanings are plainly relevant to such authoritative verbal matter as concerns Christian faith, and the difference or overlap of the two is of great importance to our main subject. The next question about authority is how far, in either sense, it requires or admits of any prior or independent determination at all; and it is suggested that it cannot rightly be treated except in the context of the whole Christian life : that is, that its prior or separate treatment, though often recommended, is of no value at all. In its place within that context, the element of authority is of great importance; but apart from it, neither verbal matter nor anything else has relevant authority for anybody. The apparently intrinsic authority of scripture, considered simply as a self-authenticating text, may seem to be an exception to this statement; but further consideration ought to show that this authority amounts to little apart from the life of the people to which the scriptures belong. It is precisely as connected with this life that the intrinsic authority of scripture amounts to anything of importance.

It is clear that all real authority in any sphere, and especially in matters of faith in God, is ultimately God's own authority; it is the question how this divine authority is mediated to men which cannot meaningfully be dealt with *a priori*. This discussion should already have thrown light on the place of verbal matter in a Christian's faith; but not much progress can be made in advance of some treatment of the specifically Christian work of the Holy Spirit in the Christian life: what does he characteristically do in this relation, and how does he do it? Chapter Three is devoted to this question: it will involve thinking about the interrelation of his work corporately in the Church, and individually in the Christian person.

In this chapter the place of written matter will have to be considered, and something will have to be said of the distinctive place of scripture in the life of the Church, though all detail about this will be left to the later chapter which is concerned entirely with scripture. How far is scripture a main *foundation* of all Christian faith and life, and how far is it rather a permanent *witness* to what that is, which has meaning only in view of the existence of that faith and life? The question of the relation of the Old and New Testaments to each other is already raised by this, but will be left for discussion in the later chapter. All that will be attempted at this stage is a general view of the relation of scripture to the Church.

Three chapters follow on three large questions which are relevant to the main subject: the first is the meaning and applicability of the commonly used concepts of infallibility and inerrancy. Can they have any meaning as applied to formulations of Christian doctrine, and if so to what matter and in what sense are they applicable? The answer suggested is that neither of them is of any use at all. It is not disputed that God is himself necessarily infallible; the question is whether he has delegated any infallibility, or any capacity to put out inerrant words. The relevance of this to the status of such words as are admittedly in some sense authoritative for Christians is too clear to need explanation.

The second question which claims a chapter is the relation of true statements to the truth about which they are statements. This could not be adequately dealt with except in a full-dress philosophical treatment which would be beyond the scope of this book; but neither could it be left out altogether. The issue is raised directly by the concept of inerrancy in words: what can be the relationship of any conceivable words to the ineffable truth of God's revelation in major matters of his divine nature and redeeming work through Christ? It will be argued that on such subjects no language is appropriate which is to be interpreted with exact literalism and can be taken as flatly factual. The revelation in scripture is conveyed in many different literary *genres,* and could not be conveyed otherwise; so must any other words on these subjects be in different ways and degrees insusceptible of exactly prosaic interpretation.

The third question is the permanent danger of hiding behind authoritative words as a secure refuge from the alarming demands of the living God. Such a procedure is taken to be what is meant by idolatry: the clinging to substitutes for the true God because you never know where you are with him. Instances of this procedure in scripture are well worth pondering when we are discussing the tendency to take scripture or other authoritative words as a talisman or a safe refuge. A distinction has to be made between an idolatrous use of God's objective gifts and the proper faithful use of them; it is not very hard to see what this difference is, but it needs to be clearly expressed and kept in mind, since scripture is an objective and definitive gift from God, as much as the Sacraments are.

At this point a transition is made to considering the main actual verbal matter with which the whole discussion is concerned. The longer of the two chapters which attempt to do this deals with Holy Scripture, and raises some of the chief questions which are relevant to estimating its authority in a Christian's faith.

Perhaps no one will be surprised to find that this is very much the longest chapter in the book, since it is plainly a much harder task to propose a satisfactory attitude to the Bible as an authoritative text than it is to propose one to Creeds or other relevant verbal matter. But it may surprise some readers to notice that this chapter begins with a sketch in some detail of the growth of the Biblical Canon, that is, of the several books of which the Bible consists. The reason for this is that without some knowledge of this process we cannot move far towards a reasonable attitude to the Bible as it came to be and now is. We could not form one by confining our attention to the finished product. Every one must assume that there is a history behind the Canon, but it is easy to disregard it if we have no idea what this history is.

The next question is how far scripture has been generally regarded as literally inerrant. It is often supposed and said that it was simply so taken until within the last two hundred years or so; but in fact the position is much less plain than that, and important distinctions have to be made.

It will be helpful at this point, though it will not at once solve all the difficulties, if the question is asked whether there are indeed errors of fact in scripture. It seems that, unless we assume *a priori* that there cannot be any, we must admit that there are many of them; and if so it is no part of God's intention in giving us the scriptures to give us exact factual reportage in all matters dealt with in them. If not, what is the meaning of saying that scripture contains just what God meant it to contain, not approximately but completely?

Two things are always believed about scripture by Christians : that it mediates God's revelation, and that it is inspired by God. The first of these things is a much more fruitful topic than the second, and more will be said about it. It is especially important to consider how far the words *are* the revelation, and how far they simply record or point authoritatively to it, without actually constituting it by themselves. This question is indeed so wide and complicated that no claim can be made to having treated it satisfactorily; but perhaps enough will be said to place the main issues in front of people who know they ought to think about it.

Since scripture will be admitted by any one who is likely to read this book at all to be incapable of proper interpretation simply by itself, some discussion must follow about its relation now to the Church, so far as its authority is concerned. What is, in its chief features, the relation between the authoritative functions of the Church and of scripture respectively? Again, it will not be possible to attempt more in this matter than to raise the main issues which call for thought.

Next, a short list of questions is mentioned which are raised by the admitted antinomy that while scripture contains just what

God means it to contain, yet much in it is very far from clear, and has in fact always caused disputes among Christians. The points mentioned under this head may well have the appearance of an arbitrary selection; and perhaps they are only not arbitrary in the sense that the writer thought them the points most worth specific mention.

A section follows about some of the main leading principles used in the exegesis of scripture. Most of these have to allow for the difficulty that documents as ancient as the books of scripture simply cannot convey their meaning to us to-day in exactly the same way as they did when they were written, or at any intermediate time. On what general lines can we interpret without avoidable falsification of meaning? Here too only a few of the relevant lines of thought can actually be referred to; but these may probably help further thinking on the subject.

This chapter on scripture will have extended to such a length that it calls for a few generalizations at the end of it, chiefly about the limited sense in which our Christian faith may be said to *depend on* scripture.

The other of the two chapters about the verbal matter which has authority for Christians deals with non-scriptural words: an attempt is made to assign to different classes of text different degrees and kinds of authority. The principle on which this is done will have been perceived long before this stage in the discussion by any reader who has not been merely skimming it: the degree of authority varies directly with the degree in which the text in question is accepted as a classical expression of the living and continuous belief of the Church. This criterion is not easy to apply, at least in some cases; but it must be, according to the whole line of thought throughout this book, the determining principle.

The final chapter, apart from the few words of conclusion which follow it, will be the discussion of heresy and schism referred to above. It will help us to understand what is meant by willing conformity with the whole life and work of the Church if attention is briefly directed to the two main forms in which this conformity can be refused: refusal in doctrine and refusal in allegiance.

CHAPTER II

AUTHORITY

IT is the aim of this chapter to attempt a general discussion of the meanings of the word Authority, so far as they are relevant to Christian faith; and further to place it in its right relation to the rest of our Christian life and thought. We shall be thinking at this stage of Authority as it is an abstract noun, and not separately of its application to individuals, as when we say 'he is an authority on geology,' to books, as when we say 'Codex B is an important authority for the text of the New Testament,' or to corporate bodies, as in the title 'Port of London Authority.' Such uses of the word are extensions of its abstract sense or senses. Nor are we concerned with any etymological investigation, as for instance with the fact that *auctor* in Latin means primarily an originator, so that attribution of *auctoritas* should provide an answer to the question 'Who says so?'

In ordinary English usage, as a dictionary will show, the word Authority has two senses, which however are closely connected and indeed overlap, particularly in their application to the main theme of our discussion. The first is, in its simplest formulation, the right or power to enforce obedience, the right to command or to take action. In Latin this is *potestas,* as in the phrase *patria potestas,* or *imperium,* as in *imperium proconsulare.* It is in this sense that we speak of the authority of the Statute Law, or, in a very different sphere, of the authority of the M.C.C. in controlling the rules of cricket.

In the other main sense of the word, Authority may be defined as power to influence action, opinion, or belief: as weight of judgment or opinion; as intellectual influence; or as title to be believed. In this sense we may say that we believe vaccination to be an effective protection against smallpox, on the authority of those who know the evidence for this belief, have practical experience of the effects of vaccination, and recommend its use, even though they have no legal right at all to enforce it. This is the Latin *auctoritas,* or at least it is a legitimate meaning of that word; and it will often conduce to clarity if in the course of our discussion we may make use of the respective Latin words to distinguish the two main senses of the English word authority.

The difference between the two senses is by now sufficiently clear : one is a legal or quasi-legal right or power, and the other is a rational ground for accepting an opinion, belief, statement, or point of view, and for acting upon it. It is when we begin to think about the relation between the two meanings that the complication and difficulties become evident.

First, we have a moral obligation to defer to authority of both kinds; yet it is not quite the same kind of obligation in the two cases. The obligation to defer to legitimate *imperium* may depend on the principle that 'there is no authority except from God, and those that exist have been instituted by God' (Rom. 13: 1, R.S.V.). This is directly true of the *imperium* of the state as it bears upon us through Common and Statute Law, the judiciary, or the police. The same kind of *imperium* bears on us, in a real though less peremptory way, in all the more serious common usages and conventions of the society in which we live; and these vary greatly both in kind and in obligatoriness, so that, though it is easy to give instances of them, they can hardly be graded in any order of importance. Thus conformity with current usage in speaking and writing has some imperative force; so have many of the conventions of public and social courtesy. Thus, to take a trivial instance, we have an obligation, in writing a letter to a clergyman of a denomination which we may believe to be wholly bogus, to put 'Reverend' on the envelope. This obligation, so far as it goes, is altogether *imperium*, and not *auctoritas*; for the weight of informed opinion may well suggest that he deserves a very different title. There is a somewhat similar force in the *imperium* already referred to, of the M.C.C. in controlling the rules of cricket. If one is concerned at all with cricket, there is a public and social ground for deferring to this *imperium*.

The moral obligation, in its varying degrees, of deferring to *imperium* is obvious enough; and the point of the preceding paragraph was rather to show that it is not confined to the authority of the state. It may perhaps sometimes be supposed that deference to *auctoritas* involves no corresponding moral obligation; but a little thought will show us that in fact it does. For there is always a moral obligation to seek and accept knowledge and truth wherever we may have access to it, and there is the same obligation to act upon it when it is possible for us to do so. Many people would perhaps say that this is a different kind of moral obligation from that imposed by *imperium*; but, at least at this stage of the argument, there is no need to discuss this difference, if it exists. We shall agree that to refuse to accept truth, when it is presented to us on adequate *auctoritas*, and deals with any matter with which we are at all concerned, is sinful. This is because all truth is God's truth, and he teaches us what we need to know of it through the *auctoritas* of those who know it already. The authority of the expert in witnessing to the truth which God has taught him is a no less real one than the authority of the Christian Church in witnessing to the Gospel itself, however inferior it may perhaps be in certainty or in importance.

The Church plainly exercises both *imperium* and *auctoritas*: for instance, we keep Sunday as a weekly holy day because of its *imperium*, and we believe that Baptism regenerates infants because of its *auctoritas*. It would be easy to think of instances in which both kinds of authority are involved, as they plainly are in the case of the Nicene Creed; but any discussion of the authority of the Church in particular would be out of place at this stage in the argument.

The question whether the Church's authority in either kind is ever absolute and beyond all criticism is one with which we shall be greatly concerned later on; indeed it has provided a main motive for the writing of this book. But at least there is little doubt that no other authority, whether *imperium* or *auctoritas*, is ever absolute, so that there can be no occasions on which deference to it is to be refused. It was to a body, the Jewish Sanhedrin, holding a real and legitimate *imperium* that St. Peter refused obedience, and protested 'We must obey God rather than men' (Acts 5 : 29); and the same is true of most martyrs in the course of the Church's history, not least of those recent ones who were killed for their Christian faith in the concentration camps of Germany, such as Dietrich Bonhöffer and Paul Schneider. There must always be an appeal to *conscience*, since the only

B

absolute and final authority is that of God himself, and we must follow what we believe to be the command of God, at whatever cost to ourselves in inconvenience or suffering.

Nevertheless, we are not to excuse ourselves on this plea from doing all we can to inform our consciences rightly, and it is the mark of a fool to assume readily that commands given under a legitimate *imperium* are to be disobeyed. Nothing can justify it, at least in any serious matter, except a clear conviction that God's command to us is otherwise; and even then we must have asked ourselves seriously whether our apparent conviction may be in fact a mistaken one. Some of those whom we honour as martyrs may well have been in some respects mistaken in the conscientious conviction which they rightly followed. A wise authority holding *imperium* will often respect the convictions of those whom it believes to be in error. St. Paul in Romans 14 gives us a pattern of this in respect of those who had conscientious scruples about eating animal food; and again in 1 Cor. 8 in respect of those whose conscience was hurt by any one eating meat which had been offered in a heathen temple. Modern governments have often followed his advice in regard to military conscription, vaccination, or the obligation to call in a qualified doctor in cases of danger to life.

The obligation to defer to *auctoritas* is equally, though rather differently, subject to an appeal to conscience. We have pointed out that there is a moral obligation to accept truth when we have an opportunity of attaining it upon adequate authority (*auctoritas*). But this implies that we have to judge of the authority's adequacy, and may be obliged in conscience to reject it. It is no doubt true that in dealing with *auctoritas* we are more obviously concerned with an intellectual than with a moral appraisal, whereas with *imperium* the converse is the case. But it will not do to make any sharp distinction between the two kinds of judgment: indeed there can be no serious moral judgment which is not also an intellectual one, and the converse is even more plainly true. To say this is more than merely to say that an accurate and careful estimation of the evidence for truth is morally obligatory upon us, so far as our abilities qualify us to make it, and that it is God who calls on us to assimilate it for use in his service. It implies all that, and something more as well:

that the actual appraisal of *auctoritas* is itself a moral as well as an intellectual procedure. There can be a culpably flippant way of appraising it.

It may be important for us to think carefully, not only about the close interrelation of the two kinds of authority, but also about the fact that all real authority in either kind is conferred by God. If we do not, we may fall into an error which has caused much erroneous theory and practice, especially at the Reformation in the sixteenth century. This is the view that there are only two holders of *imperium* appointed by God, the Church and the State, and that problems of authority need consideration only when the claims of these two *imperia* may conflict. Some-times an application of the biblical text about the two swords has been made to support this view. It ignores not only the fact that other kinds of *imperium* in human society are real, and are held under a providential divine appointment; but also the whole realm of *auctoritas* as it also is conferred by God and therefore imposes obligations no less important. It is always bad reasoning to counter an argument by bringing in trivial cases; but on this topic it may seem particularly plausible to do so, and therefore the caution may be in place. It will not do, for instance, to imagine that any point is scored by asking whether God has appointed the referee to his job on every football field; though in fact it ought to be answered that he *has,* and that no one is entitled to laugh except those who think that God is concerned only with mighty matters.

It may be expected that some discussion should be included about the distinction between authority for belief and authority for practice; but this distinction, however obvious, is superficial, and is in no way to be equated with the distinction between *imperium* and *auctoritas.* Though the former is often most plainly a right to command that something should be done, it is seldom exclusively so. In any well-governed society, whether state, school, club, or any other, a legitimate order to do some-thing affords in some degree a reason for the belief that this thing is good, or at least expedient. In other words, *imperium* com-monly involves *auctoritas* as well. Again there may be a tempta-tion to counter with trivial instances: we may be asked what belief is commended by a notice 'Please keep off the grass.' The answer is that it is of course no belief of grave importance, but none the less that such a notice is, in a well-governed municipality, a reason for believing that the place will look better if the grass is not walked on. It would be more helpful to point out, for instance, that the contents of Statute Law have *auctoritas* in a high degree, as affording grounds for acceptance of much that is wise and true.

In the converse case, acceptance of *auctoritas* often involves an obligation to do something about what is accepted as true, as well as the simple duty of accepting it. In the case quoted above, of the *auctoritas* on which we accept the belief that vaccination is an effective protection against smallpox, there is the duty of having ourselves vaccinated, as well as of intellectually accepting its efficacy. Acceptance of truth on *auctoritas* almost always involves some duty of practice as well as of accepting belief.

The upshot of the discussion so far may seem to be that the whole distinction between *imperium* and *auctoritas,* with which we began, has become blurred and confused. But something still remains of it : an order to be obeyed is not the same thing as a reason for a belief or a practice. Throughout this book it will often be relevant to bear this distinction in mind, as well as the fact that each of the two implies some degree of the other. It has already been made clear that in the case of the Church's authority the distinction is at its least sharp, and the mutual implication at its plainest. Truth and wisdom are to be learnt from what the Church commands, and some sort of a command to act is involved in what comes to us on the Church's teaching *auctoritas*. The media of the Church's authority, and the degree and kind of authoritativeness they carry, are a main theme of this book, and no anticipation of this subject is in place at this stage of the discussion. The other subject which ought to be raised now is the place, or priority in place, of the question of authority in relation to the rest of our life as members of the Church.

It was pointed out in the preceding panoramic chapter that the Church's authority in matters of belief and practice is often regarded and urged upon us as a kind of preliminary topic about which every Christian must first of all be very definite in order to be able to live as a rational Christian at all. It is from more than one quarter that we are told that the question where this authority lies has this fundamental and even separable character. The way in which this view of authority is pressed upon us is in many respects similar, whether it is a Roman Catholic or a conservative Evangelical that we are talking to. Both will press the question on us as in some way primary, though their respective answers to it are of course different; and we may well find that the Roman Catholic's answer coheres a good deal better with the rest of what he has to say to us than the Evangelical's answer does. It coheres better with his whole system, especially as it concerns teaching on doctrine and practice. But in one respect the two answers to what both regard as a primary question are very much alike : both assume that what we are looking for, and must be able to find, is a source of final and formulated truths, available for permanent and definitive reference. They suggest that if we do not have this prior clarity we are all at sea and without any sure guidance at all about faith or morals. Even if we are sure ourselves that this is not at all the sort of thing God has given us, and that it is incompatible with what we know of the working of the Holy Spirit in the Church and in individual Christians, we are none the less bound to treat this view seriously, since it is held in some form by very many Christians, and can be plausibly presented as in some sense the traditional view. We are not, for example, to argue against it by a *reductio ad absurdum*, or to dismiss it by quoting the whimsical dictum of W. G. Ward, 'I should like a new papal Bull every morning with my *Times* at breakfast' (Wilfrid Ward, *William George Ward and the Catholic Revival*, p. 14).

So long as we make the two prior assumptions (a) that we must look for some identifiable source of formulated truths, recourse to which is easy and always definitive, and (b) that until we have found this we have no prospect of a rational Christian life, then some such answer as the Roman Catholic gives us in one form and the conservative Evangelical in another is reasonable enough. On these two assumptions, the Roman Catholic may say something like this : You are looking for a source of definitive truths in the form of statements; if such truths are to be relevant to what you now want to know, they must come from a Church which both issues them, and claims infallibility in doing so; there is no Church which does this except the Roman Catholic Church; therefore you ought to become a Roman Catholic. No doubt the argument will not be put as baldly as this, but given the two initial assumptions it is not an unreasonable argument in principle, and it coheres in detail with what one is afterwards taught, if one has accepted it and become a Roman Catholic.

The conservative Evangelical may argue as J. I. Packer does in his able book, *'Fundamentalism' and the Word of God*. He there says (p. 42) 'The problem of authority is the most fundamental problem that the Christian Church ever faces. This is because Christianity is built on truth : that is to say, on the content of a divine revelation.' He goes on later (p. 43) '. . . we see how important it is to find a right criterion of truth, by which we may tell the word of God from human error.' And on the following page we read 'This being so, we must not be surprised that the problem of authority still divides Christian people. And clearly it is the most far-reaching and fundamental division that there is, or can be, between them. The deepest cleavages in Christendom are doctrinal; and the deepest doctrinal cleavages are those which result from disagreement about authority. Radical divergences are only to be expected when there is no agreement about the proper grounds for believing anything.'

Clearly Packer does not mean that the question whether or not God's word is always to be obeyed constitutes a fundamental problem, for no Christian doubts this. And so far as he is here arguing that obedience to revealed truth is of the greatest importance, as against the view, once common but now rare, that our human reason can excogitate it from any sources that happen to appeal to us, his words are entirely acceptable. But his argument may well raise misgivings. First, on a question of fact, it is not major doctrinal issues which form the deepest divisions between Christians : all the important Christian communions agree, for instance, in accepting the Nicene Creed as authoritative for belief, whether or not it is their custom to recite it in public worship. What divides them are corollaries of fundamental doctrine : questions which have indeed doctrinal bearings, but are more concerned with order, jurisdiction, and the detailed interpretation of a doctrine believed by all.

What causes still more misgiving is the isolated kind of way in which Packer views the question : he presents it out of its context, as a kind of separate and preliminary question. This approach seems to be wrong, and to lead almost inevitably to a kind of crudity. It is an unhelpful approach for one who is not yet a Christian ; and for one who is, it is impossible to deal with the question of the authority or the reception of revealed truth without reference to what God has done at our baptism and since then, or to the present and living work of the Holy Spirit in the Church and in the individual member of it. The question cannot usefully be discussed by a Christian except in relation to these things. Such discussions of it as we find in Packer's book are almost bound to take what in less able writers may be called an oracular view of authority, and in his case should be called by whatever politer synonym for that term may be found. The reason for this is that when the question is treated on its own, the only alternative to some such view is an unacceptably man-centred one ; whereas if we treat it in its whole context in the life of the Church as the Body of Christ guided by the Holy Spirit, no such pair of alternatives faces us.

This suggests that our approach to the question of authority for Christian truth should follow something like the lines now to be described. We have been set by God, at our baptism, within the Church, and his authority is mediated to us in the whole context of the Church's life and activity. There is no reason for separating his authority for truth from the authority for anything else that the Church does under the guidance of his Holy Spirit. In other words, *auctoritas* for truth, and *imperium* for our acceptance of it, are not prior questions at all. They constitute an integral and important part of our total obligation to conform to and take our part in the whole of the Church's life and activity, because God has put us there and called us to do this at all times. Authority then is the source of the duty of accepting and conforming to the Church of God which believes and does what we can see and learn that it believes and does. On this view, acceptance of God's truth is not essentially different from acceptance of vocation, or indeed of any of the dispositions of his providence. We shall come later to consider how far revealed truth must be conveyed in grammatical propositions ; but it will

already be clear that there is less reason for its always being so
if we consider the subject in the whole context of the Church's
life.

There seem to be two ways in which the question may arise in
urgent form of what is authoritative within the Church, and in
what way it is so. The first concerns any one not already a Christian, who has to decide whether he is to become one. No doubt
in practice such a question hardly ever comes before any one in
a clear and isolated form at all; but theoretically it might, and
then the issue of authority certainly arises. Such a person has to
make up his mind whether the Church does authoritatively
mediate God's claim on his allegiance; and this cannot be done
without going into a good deal of detail. In the present divided
state of Christendom he will also have to decide which Christian
communion is in this respect the authentic, or the most authentic, mediator of God's authority. At least he must attempt to do
this so far as he has the ability and the opportunity to do so.
What he does *not* need to do is to seek first to arrive at some
independent criterion of the intrinsic authority of any words or
texts, whether in scripture or elsewhere, with a view to subse-
quently deciding about the Church. Some people may indeed try
to proceed in this way, and suppose it to be useful; but in fact
no such independent criterion is to be found, or could be recognized, apart from the whole context of the Church's life and
work. In independence of this, no question about what beliefs
and practices have God's authority, or in what sense they have
it, can be profitably tackled at all. Such questions can only be
answered by living within the Church, and so assimilating and
thinking out the meaning of the beliefs and practices which form
parts of its life.

This brings us to the second, and apparently only other, way
in which the question of authority can normally arise; and here
it is matters of detail which are involved. When a Christian who
is living as a member of the Church has misgivings about some
matter of belief or practice which the Church appears to maintain, he will have to consider how far such a belief or practice
is in fact authoritative within the Church. Plainly here the issue
of authority is very much a posterior question, and not a prior
one. Moreover it cannot be settled only or chiefly by assessing

the authoritativeness of this or that text or formula; though no doubt an educated Christian will include such considerations along with others. The chief task for his mind will be to see how far the matter he is worried about is in fact integral to, and constant in, the Church's life. Moreover he is engaged on something quite different from a private intellectual investigation; he will not get far unless he regards his task as one for which his first need is to pray for the guidance of the Holy Spirit, and probably his main further need is consultation of those fellow-Christians whose judgment he trusts. Once again in this case, little progress is to be attained by any prior or independent assessment of the authoritativeness of any verbal matter.

Perhaps the same single point has by now been sufficiently laboured: namely, that the Church's authoritative words, whether found in scripture or elsewhere, can only be usefully accepted or assimilated by one who is trying to live within the Church. If an attempt is made to do so otherwise, a choice of two wholly unacceptable alternatives arises: either to accept texts, scriptural or other, as interpretable by themselves, almost or quite as we interpret legal statutes; or else to take them as offered for interpretation to the independent human reason. If this is the dilemma which seems to face people, there is no wonder that the 'fundamentalist' choice is commonly preferred to the 'liberal' one. Within the Church, questions of authoritativeness normally arise only about secondary matters whose place may be doubtful or marginal, and when they do arise they are not dealt with chiefly by any literalist inspection of texts or formulae. The dilemma we have just referred to does not face us. There are indeed people, including loyal Christians, who like to have things definitively embodied in so many words; but on such matters as God's revelation they either cannot be, or ought not to be, satisfied. Such matters are mostly not capable of definitive formulation at all, because they concern the infinite God. A discussion of this is attempted below, in Chapter Five. It is also to be feared that a craving for definitive formulae on subjects which are not susceptible of them is often a sign of the temptation to idolatry, in the sense of that word which is considered in Chapter Six: namely, a faithless craving to have something easy and amenable to cling to, so as to shelter from the living God.

In any case, it is not a good sign when Christians readily or frequently ask themselves exactly how much they are committed to in the way of beliefs or practices : their whole lives and selves are committed to the service of God in the shared and common life of his Church. An analogy may be suggested here which, though only partly fair, presents at least some features parallel to the Christian's position in this respect. Suppose someone has married a girl with whom he is in love : he does not ask himself what exactly he has committed himself to by his marriage, and it is not a good sign if such a question readily comes into his mind. He has bound himself and his life to her, and gladly accepts all the implications of this fact. The loyal Christian is not apt to ask himself what exactly is authoritative within the Church, or to what degree it is so. In all ordinary circumstances, he knows he is to share the Church's life in all respects, and he accepts all that plainly belongs to it, whether belief or anything else, as having God's authority, because the Church is Christ's Body and family, in which the Holy Spirit mediates and interprets to its members God's revelation, alike for belief and for practice : as much for worship and for work as for doctrine. In fact, such questions of detail as do arise are more likely to concern practice than belief. But whatever their subject may be, we are not to expect to solve them by a simple recourse to formulae of any kind, as if these could usefully be appealed to over against the Church. That is just the sort of thing God does not give us. It would be inconsistent with what he has given us in giving us the living guidance of the Holy Spirit to control and interpret the things of Christ both in the Church and in each of its members.

The Christian has in fact all the means for solving his difficulties which God has given him, and a budget of isolable formulae is not among them. Written matter has certainly its important place among these gifts : scripture has a unique place, and the Creeds have their place. But neither scripture nor the Creeds are to be regarded as isolable blocks of definitive information which can be used by themselves. Both are to be seen rather as a permanent standing record and witness, which have use and meaning within the context of the whole life and activity of the Christian Church. It will be the task of later chapters in this book to enlarge on this description in the case of Scripture and the Creeds respectively. At this present stage in the argument, the important thing is to see that God's authority is not mediated to us through his Church in guaranteed texts which can be used by themselves as settling any question; though there are such texts which are of great use within the whole context of the Church's life.

When any question arises for the Christian about what is authoritative in belief or practice, it is not soluble by looking up the answer in the book, and finding it formulated in so many words. His procedure is to pray for the guidance of the Holy Spirit, and to consult those of his Christian friends whose judgment on such a question he thinks will be a wise one. He will also probably use written matter as well, especially his Bible and his Prayer Book; but he will resort to them as having meaning in the context of all that built-up knowledge of what his Christian faith implies which has come to him by his living in it. With these, and perhaps other, helps, he decides the question for himself as before God. He does not need, and God has not given him, a set of guaranteed statements or bye-laws which by themselves settle any doubt or question.

That is just the sort of thing God does not give us; it would be inconsistent with all he has told us in the Bible of his methods with men, and notably with what we know of our Lord's own procedure with those who brought him topical conundrums to solve. It would be inconsistent with what he *has* given us, namely personal knowledge of himself, mediated both through the Bible and the daily life of the Church, with the gift of the Holy Spirit to teach and guide every Christian person. The Bible is not a text-book, for a text-book would not teach us to know its author personally. And it is self-interpreting only in the sense that one part of it helps to interpret another part. It is by no means self-interpreting in the sense that any intellectually competent person who reads all the relevant passages objectively can assimilate all that it is capable of conveying.

In fact, none of God's gifts to his people can be thought of as operating apart from the personal work of the Holy Spirit; and for this reason the following chapter has this work for its subject. We may conclude this one with a summary of those parts of it which should be kept in mind as we proceed in our argument.

It has become clear that a main crux in the controversy about authority in our Christian faith is whether or not we ought to look primarily for texts or formulated statements at all. According to one view we ought to do this, and indeed cannot be rational Christians until we have first found out what these texts are, and have accepted them *ex animo* as they stand. When we have found them, and greeted them as definitive words of God, our task is to assimilate and understand them, and then to use them as given premises for deduction whenever we are faced with intellectual or practical problems. Our acceptance of them in this way is even taken as the only respectable intellectual ground of our being Christians at all, and the Church is understood largely as the body which maintains and helps us to enter into the meaning of such texts.

The alternative view, which this book seeks to commend, is that Christian authority is primarily another name for the obligation arising from God's having made us Christians; the obligation, namely, to assimilate ourselves to every part and aspect of the Church's life, work, and belief. Within the whole context of this there are indeed texts having authority, as there are equally Sacraments, morals, and practices having it. But the authority of these texts is not absolute, external, or prior: the texts are part of what we learn to know and use as 'very members incorporate' in God's Christian Church.

The antithesis is often presented as an alternative between an oracular and a non-oracular view of authoritative texts; but this is not a fair way of stating it. It is still less fair when it is stated, in the interest of the other side, as a contrast between a humble and docile attitude and an arrogantly critical one. The question is rather whether the intellectual ground of our Christian faith is primarily a set of texts or statements at all, and if it is not, what place ought to be assigned to authoritative texts or statements. This is the question to which the following chapters are meant to help in providing an answer. The general line which this answer will take is that the main clue is in our having been chosen by God and placed within the fellowship of his Church, to whose belief and practice we willingly assimilate ourselves under the guidance of the Holy Spirit. All that the Church believes and practises is in some degree authoritative, because the Church is what it is : the people of God and the Body of Christ. There are indeed degrees of authoritativeness, and some consideration of them will have to be attempted in subsequent chapters.

Meanwhile, our next task must be to think about the Holy Spirit and the Church; when we do this we shall see that we are concerned primarily with his corporate and individual work in people, and only subordinately with his having authorized or inspired authoritative words.

CHAPTER III

THE HOLY SPIRIT AND THE CHURCH

WE have said in the preceding chapter that if authority for belief in Christian truth is taken as a kind of preliminary topic by itself, one is likely to be driven into the dilemma of taking either a mechanical and oracular view of Scripture and other authoritative texts or else an unacceptably man-centred view. In its extreme form, this dilemma would present a choice of saying either that God has issued, and perhaps now issues, inerrant propositions to teach and guide us, or else that we have no effective guidance at all about truth, beyond what human reason by itself can reach. The dilemma is in fact seldom presented to us in so crude a form as this, but some qualified form of it is not uncommonly found; we find it, for instance in J. I. Packer's book already referred to, *'Fundamentalism' and the Word of God.*

The escape from this dilemma will involve our thinking about authority for truth in its proper context, namely the context of what God has done in making the Catholic Church, incorporating us as members of it, and controlling and guiding both it and its members by his Holy Spirit. If the question of authoritative truth is regarded in its place within this context, there is no need to take an oracular view as the only alternative to a purely man-centred one. The former is not indeed excluded, for God might have issued such oracles in addition to the rest of what he has done; and many Christians have supposed that he has. But we are not bound to suppose it; and what we know of the work of his Holy Spirit in the Church and in its members will certainly rule out the idea that we have no authority for truth beyond unaided human reason.

The subject of the Holy Spirit and the Church is far too large to tackle in one chapter; but some important aspects of it may be shortly considered.

On the view outlined in the preceding chapter, the Christian grows in his assimilation and understanding of revealed truth very much as he does in his assimilation and understanding of prayer, worship, morals, and practical witness. He does all this by becoming identified with the Church's life and work in all its aspects, as the Holy Spirit the Paraclete guides him, within the Church, 'into all the truth' (St. John 16 : 13).

There is a likely objection here, that, whatever may be the case with other authoritative words, Holy Scripture at least has an authority relatively independent of God's other gifts and operations in the Church, since the Church appeals to it to prove other things. This has been the case with the Old Testament from the first preaching of the Gospel, and with the New Testament as well ever since its canon was established. But Scripture has never been an independent standard, over against the Church; it always stands as the Church's witness to the testimony of our Lord's Apostles, and its canon was fixed by and within the Church to preclude deviations from the one and only Gospel. This fixing of the canon of Scripture implied a recognition of the uniqueness and finality of the Apostolic witness, and of the facts to which witness was borne, and of the meaning always attributed to those facts.

It is true that, by this fixing of the canon, Scripture is recognized as a permanent norm to which all the Church's teaching must conform. But that is not to recognize Scripture as an independent standard over against the Church; it is to recognize it as a permanent witness to the one Gospel which from the first the Church has proclaimed, and must continue to proclaim. The function of any later appeal to Scripture is to show that what is now taught agrees with what has been taught from the first. Further discussion of Scripture within the Church will be attempted in Chapter Seven. What has been said here is meant simply to put aside the objection that Scripture at least is an independently authoritative standard. It is so in a sense which will need further discussion; but not in any sense which makes against the argument of this chapter.

To continue this argument, it will be necessary now to consider the work of the Holy Spirit in relation to the Church, both as regards the Church's nature, and as regards its teaching and the gifts with which God has endowed it. Holy Scripture is one such gift, but there are others as well : the Sacraments, the inspiration of prayer and public worship, and the discernment of

God's will here and now. The infallibilist view of Scripture will
call for a fuller discussion in Chapter Seven, but it is relevant at
the present stage because its plausibility comes largely from taking Scripture too much as a thing on its own, out of its context
in the life and tradition of the Church, and in too little relation
to the guidance of the Holy Spirit by which that life and tradition is at every time continued and inspired.

When those who take this view speak of the inspiration of
Scripture, they commonly mean the inspiration by virtue of
which it was *composed,* and they give much less attention to the
work of the Holy Spirit in guiding its reading and interpretation
by Christian people. In the main, the early Church took exactly
the opposite line : they say and think much of reading and interpreting Scripture under the guidance of the Holy Spirit, and less
of his work in guiding its original composition, although this idea
is not altogether absent.

Our immediate aim now is to look at the work of the Holy
Spirit as we find it regarded in the New Testament, in order to
see the place within this work of Scripture and of such other
authoritative matter as is considered to be in some way 'taught'
by the Spirit. This will involve what may seem to some the odd
procedure of discussing the Bible and the Church together, before
discussing the Bible itself as an authoritative text. The reason is
that the second subject cannot be tackled sensibly till the first
has been dealt with : if it is tackled outside this context, some
sort of infallibilist view of it may well seem acceptable.

Indeed, before we can fairly consider the place and authority
to be assigned to the Bible as a text, we shall have to interpose
three more chapters after this one ; and only then shall we be in
a position to assess it, though important principles needed for
this assessment will have emerged during the intervening process.
The three subjects which will then have been discussed will be :
first, the concept of infallibility as applied to persons, and of inerrancy as applied to words, secondly the relationship of true
words to the truth, and thirdly the danger and the attractiveness
of using words or texts as idols. By idols is meant more amenable
substitutes for the living God.

We have already said that to suppose God to have given us a
wholly inerrant record in words, to which appeal may be made

by itself, is to suppose something which does not well accord with what we know of the Holy Spirit's methods of working, and is perhaps even incompatible with them. This judgment needs to be supported by some account of what we do know from the New Testament of his methods of working.

It is to be hoped that no one will wish at this point to object that this procedure amounts to appealing to the New Testament in order to argue against the inerrancy of the New Testament. For we shall be assuming no more at this stage than this, that the New Testament, whether verbally inerrant or not, gives us the best evidence about the characteristic ways in which the Holy Spirit works, both in the Church corporately and in individual Christians. The conclusion is to be that his known ways of working do not encourage us to suppose that he has also inspired an inerrant textual record to which some sort of isolated appeal can be made. In broader terms, that the authority of the Bible makes sense only in the context in which it was written, as addressed to the people of God, and not if it is taken as isolable from this context.

There is no inconsistency at all between saying this and at the same time recognizing that every reformation within the Church has always founded itself upon an appeal to the Bible ; for these appeals have never been made to the Bible as an independent text, but always to the Bible as a standing witness to what is admittedly the Church's normal belief or practice.

The New Testament has its own distinctive view of the characteristic work of the Holy Spirit under and in relation to the Christian Gospel. This view is not a simple development or continuation of the Old Testament's conception of the Spirit of the Lord ; indeed, we are plainly told in St. John's Gospel that upon the basis of our Lord's saving work a new and characteristic gift of the Holy Spirit is to begin. In this sense, during the earthly ministry, 'as yet the Spirit had not been given, because Jesus was not yet glorified' (St. John 7 : 39). In the Old Testament the Spirit of the Lord means usually an endowment of power or ability from God, in virtue of which a man or a body of men can do or say what they could not have done or said by their normal human powers. None of this is denied in the New Testament; but the distinctively Christian gift of the Spirit is something new, and different from it.

C

Indeed, in the Old Testament the distinction between the Spirit and the Word of God is not very clear; it hardly could be so until 'the Word became flesh, and dwelt among us.' Once this had happened, the distinction always observed in the New Testament became clear: the Word is always the object and the content of God's gift to man, and of all his self-expression in and to his creation. The Spirit is always the interpreter and the realizer of the Word. In the Old Testament the Word of God is his speech, his communication, to men, whether for information about his will or for charging men with the task of declaring it to others, as is the case with the prophets. In the later parts of the Old Testament, his Word also means the act whereby he created the world and its contents. All this is taken up and re-interpreted in the New Testament and all of it is recognized as true of that eternal Word, the Son of God, who had been made Man.

In the New Testament the Spirit, as distinctively given after our Lord's saving work, is always the interpreter and the realizer of Christ to men. He has no distinctive function at all apart from this context of Christ's Person, work, and teaching. In the Gospels, our Lord is himself the bearer of the Spirit; St. Mark in particular emphasizes this fact. He is also the bestower of the Spirit upon his Church after he himself is exalted. Most of the clearest passages about this are found in the fourteenth, fifteenth, and sixteenth chapters of St. John's Gospel; but the rest of the New Testament provides nothing at variance with it. The Holy Spirit's sole specifically Christian function is always to interpret and to bear witness to the things of Christ, both inwardly to the Church and the Church's members, and outwardly through the Church to 'the world' which does not believe. We find this teaching most clearly in the following passages of St. John's Gospel: 14: 16, 17 and 26; 15: 26 and 27; 16: 7 to 15. When it is said of the Paraclete that 'he shall guide you into all the truth,' the reference is to that truth which 'came by Jesus Christ' (St. John 1 : 17). The same teaching may be found in St. Paul's Epistles in such passages as Galatians 4: 4 to 6; Romans 5: 5, and 1 Corinthians 12 : 3; and it is taken up again in the first Epistle of St. John at 4: 1 to 3.

It seems true to say that the New Testament knows nothing of the Holy Spirit in his work under the Christian Gospel apart from this function. It is specifically by the Spirit that Christians know Christ and have the mind of Christ. Apart from the Spirit, we should have no more of Christ than an impersonal memory. The Spirit is the controller and interpreter to whom the Church and all Christians are permanently subject by obedience. He is therefore not the successor to Christ, nor the independent guarantor of anything other than the person and work of Christ. Christ reigns in the world, and mediates himself to the world, by the personal operation of the Holy Spirit, particularly through the Church.

When all this has been said and admitted, no proof has been offered that the Holy Spirit has not also, and independently of his normal kind of work for Christians, inspired an inerrant verbal text to guide and teach us, or that he has not also given us at later times inerrant definitions through Councils, Popes, or otherwise. The only profitable way to reach a conclusion about whether he has or not is to look at these texts and see whether they seem to have this character or not. It is clear that many Christians in the past and at present think they, or some of them, have, and that many others have not thought so. There is certainly no such unanimity on the subject that catholic loyalty obliges us to suppose it. The present argument does no more than tend to show that, if he has, he has done something very different from what we know of his normal ways of working in the Church and in individual members of it.

We shall be more inclined to look at Scripture, and perhaps at the Creeds, as records of the Spirit's interpreting witness to Christ, a witness to be accepted in the whole context of his operation to this effect; and not as definitive texts of a more or less oracular character standing over against that operation. To take this view is not to deny that Scripture may be called in a true and important sense 'the word of God,' though it suggests that it would be misleading to call it 'the words of God.' For any specific call or challenge addressed by God to men is certainly God's word : any definite communication from him to us is so. Very many different things have been meant by calling Scripture 'the word of God,' and they will have to be sorted out in Chapter Seven; but there is no need at all to refuse the phrase on the ground that its use implies a capitulation to a fundamentalist view of Scripture. At the very least, Scripture is a medium through which the Holy Spirit witnesses to Christ, both to the Church corporately and to individual Christians at every time when they reverently read it. Apart from the Spirit's so using it, Scripture remains inert : this can be well seen in the inept comments it evokes from well-intentioned unbelievers, and in another way by the extraordinary things found in it by cranks and the spokesmen of sects. These people are often devout and unselfish, but they do not accept 'authority' in the sense outlined in the previous chapter, where it was described as the obligation to conform ourselves with the whole life of the catholic and apostolic Church. Outside this context, Scripture will be made to mean some very odd things. This fact also seems to support the general argument of this chapter.

Again, support is being gained for the statement already made that the important function of the Spirit in relation to Scripture has to do rather with its reading and interpretation than with its original composition as a text by itself. It seems to be only in modern times, indeed in times later than those of the great reformers of the sixteenth century, that the latter question has tended to replace the former. There is no doubt a question about the relation of the Spirit to the first writing of the scriptural books, and it will need discussion before we have done; but it is not the primary question.

It seems certainly fair to assume that no part of Scripture, indeed no detail in it, is superfluous or irrelevant to God's purpose in providing us with it. But what internal characteristics this may imply is a question not soluble *a priori* at all, and one to which no clear answer is to be found in catholic tradition and consent. Different analogies have at different times affected Christian thought on the subject, and some review of them will have to be attempted later in this book. We cannot begin with an agreed answer, even if any wholly satisfactory answer is attainable at all.

The present argument is that the Spirit is God's personal and controlling influence by which Christians enter into, understand, and live by, all the objective gifts of the Gospel. These gifts certainly include Scripture ; they also include, for instance, his personal guidance and indeed self-expression (Romans 8 : 26) in all our prayer. He is the Spirit of adoption by which we cry 'Abba, Father' (Romans 8 : 15). He also operates in us by the Sacraments, chiefly in Baptism and in the Holy Communion. Always he points us to the person and work of Christ, teaches us what they mean, and activates in us all the blessings and gifts which they convey.

We are right in distinguishing, for certain purposes, his work in the Church corporately from his work in individuals; but in both his operation is emphatically a personal one. And this is to distinguish it from his general operation in all created things whether animate or inanimate. The former is commonly called 'grace,' and the latter has been technically called *concursus generalis*. In the Old Testament the distinction is implied, but not clearly drawn : he 'spoke through the prophets,' and we also read 'When thou sendest forth thy Spirit, they are created' (Psalm 104 : 30).

Something should now be said of the former distinction, between the Spirit's continuing personal work in the corporate Church on the one hand, and in the individual Christian on the other. Clearly they interact at every point; and no less clearly the former is not merely a summation of the latter. There is a common corporate mind of the Church, guided through the ages of its history, and also at the present time, by the Holy Spirit. Some people think that this common mind is known, and has been recorded, in certain texts to which a special kind of inerrancy attaches. They may add the rider that little can be known of it apart from such an assumed inerrancy. The argument of this book does not so much deny this notion as call it wrongly stated. It is indeed true that the Church regards some texts as final, in the sense that they will never be due for replacement; the Creeds are an obvious instance of such texts. But their finality does not rest on their having been issued by some special kind of body of people who met under an *a priori* guarantee that it was competent to issue inerrant words. It rests on the fact that the Church has certainly accepted them as normative; and if this fact may mean calling some texts more definitive than others, and not allow us to draw a sharp line between wholly inerrant ones and those which may contain mistakes, a belief in the present teaching work of the Holy Spirit will save us from being disconcerted. This will still be true, even if we find we can attach no clear meaning to the term inerrancy or infallibility as applied to texts.

The Spirit has also guided, and still guides, the Church in much other teaching, less obviously embodied in texts at all : for instance about the meaning of Scripture, about the Sacraments, and about morals. He has no less certainly guided the Church in the tradition of the practice of prayer, of public worship, and in its work and witness in the world. All this teaching and practical guidance is indeed in a true sense based on Holy Scripture, though often not plainly or unequivocally. The words of our own Articles VI and XX are wise, both in what they say and in what they refrain from saying. Article VI says : 'Holy Scripture containeth all things necessary to salvation : so that whatsoever is not read therein, nor may be proved thereby, is not to be required of any man, that it should be believed as an article of the Faith, or be thought requisite or necessary to salvation.' And Article XX says : ' . . . It is not lawful for the Church to ordain any thing that is contrary to God's Word written, neither may it so expound one place of Scripture, that it be repugnant to another.' Outside and beyond such things as are in this sense contained in Scripture the Church must exercise, and always has exercised, an *imperium* which in all normal circumstances claims the obedience of every loyal member for the very reason that he is a loyal member.

In all such matters the Church's teaching and guidance, though not contained in or to be proved by Scripture, is none the less the Church's understanding of what is implied by, or consonant with Scripture, in respect of the Church's belief, worship, work, and witness. A loyal member of the Church will neither want nor look for any exact criterion by which to judge exactly what he is committed to in any of these matters : again, for the very reason that he is a loyal member of the Church. This point has been sufficiently dealt with in the preceding chapter. He has, and is amply content with, the Church's living tradition about what is grounded in Holy Scripture, and has no need or temptation to ask for an independently guaranteed list of inerrant sentences. The question of whether there is any useful meaning to be attached to the concept of infallibility or of in-

errancy in matters concerning the revelation given to men by
God is the subject of the chapter which follows this one. All that
is now being said is that there is at least normally no need of any
such concepts.

It is often supposed that on many matters the Church has
infallibly expressed its mind in particular inerrant formulae. All
Roman Catholics since 1870, and many of them long before that
date, have believed that the Pope has promulgated words of this
kind, though the more careful ones gives us only a very short
list indeed of such utterances. Many English churchmen of an
earlier generation have attributed a similar status to the definitions put out by some General Councils, either the first four, the
first six, or the first seven of them; and perhaps the same view
is occasionally held today. The view maintained in this book is
that the authority of such definitions is based on their expressing
in classical form the guided mind of the Church, so far as they
do in fact express this; it does not, in our view, depend upon
any *a priori* assumption that such and such definitions must be
inerrant because they were put out, by the authority which made
them, under conditions which made it certain that it would be
empowered by God to utter inerrant sentences.

The continuing work of the Holy Spirit in individual Christians has much bearing on our subject, since its reality and
effectiveness provides one main reason why we do not need to
depend for guidance upon inerrant formulae handed to us, so
to speak, from outside. The relevance of this continuing work
to the authority of Scripture is not so much in its bearing upon
the composition of Scripture—the belief that its writers were
inspired when they wrote—but rather as it bears upon the reading and understanding of Scripture by Christians now. Not only
is there a living corporate tradition in the Church about the way
Scripture is to be interpreted, but also at every time God speaks
through Scripture to individuals as his Spirit guides them in their
reading of it. Hence the well-known difficulty of saying exactly
what is meant by calling Scripture 'the Word of God.' The
willingness to use this phrase of Scripture has sometimes become
almost a party slogan within the Church; it is extremely ill fitted
for this use, because almost all orthodox Christians will accept it
in some senses and reject it in others.

The individual Christian, as he is personally guided in his reading and understanding of Scripture by the Holy Spirit, never forgets the context in which Scripture is given to him : he reads it always as one whose whole life is that of a member of the Church, with a living share in its worship and witness as much as in its belief. In every part of his life as a Christian, there is a balance to be preserved between loyal conformity with the Church as a body and the individual initiative without which his self-identification with the Church would be no more than a lifeless one. No Christian can be a loyal member of the Church who considers himself exempt from the obligation to use his own mind, heart, and will to understand, love, and join heartily in all the Church's life, *as he can see it for himself.* Very much more is always needed for the intellectual part of this process than to accept verbal matter as definitive, and the question remains whether to do this is a part of it at all.

The most characteristic activity of the Holy Spirit in individual Christians is, in general, his teaching them to discern the will of God in every daily choice that faces them. Normally, he enlightens them so that they discern God's will for themselves; and he does this by enabling them to make use concurrently of Scripture, of the consensus of Christian tradition, and of the advice of any other Christian people whom they may care to consult. It is not, so far as we know, his way to teach us only by referring us to a definitive answer in verbal form, whether in Scripture or in some collection of doctrinal texts; though no doubt we shall often include a consideration of texts in our deliberations.

In other words, the best human analogy to the normal working of the Holy Spirit in teaching and guidance is the personal influence of a wise friend. Any such influence is necessarily effective only so far as it is attended to : so far as it is not attended to, it might as well not exist for us. Our friend may indeed influence us through what he writes; but pointing to already existing words is not at all the characteristic method by which one person's influence on another is conveyed.

There is no need at this point to introduce yet one more discussion about the interrelation of the Bible and the Church, which might well exasperate a reader who has already seen too many such discussions. If our general theological principles are sound, the relationship is clear enough : we shall remember the place of the Church in the Creeds, which is an eschatological place. The Church in this world is not the Church completed and glorified, though it is rightly described as the Body of Christ. But this description cannot be used to disguise the imperfection of its constitutional embodiment here and now. The Church is *being* taught by the Holy Spirit, and is *being* led into all the truth ; and the truth into which it is being led is that which came fully and definitively in Jesus Christ. So neither is the present Church lord over Scripture, nor conversely is a separately interpretable Scripture lord over the Church. Both are in different ways means by which the Holy Spirit teaches and perfects his work in those whom God has in Christ elected and incorporated as his own children. The Church has, under the Holy Spirit's guidance, recognized Scripture as its norm for both belief and practice.

If there is any antinomy here, it has no puzzling consequences for loyal Christians now, unless indeed they are contemplating a change of religious allegiance from one communion to another. If they are contemplating this step, they are under a great temptation to absolutize either the one or the other, in order to help themselves by finding absolute directives from the Bible or from the Church. It will be suggested in the chapter on idolatry (Chapter Six) that God does not provide us with either of these easy ways, or with any other easy way, of avoiding that openness to his particular demands on us which faith continually requires of us in this world. He has indeed provided us with known means through which he will always teach us and guide us into the knowledge of his will in matters alike of belief and of practice. Among these means, Scripture has its essential place in relation to the Church, and so has the Church in relation to Scripture. But to set the one in opposition to the other is always a capital mistake ; nor do the two in conjunction afford us any rule of thumb by which we may answer our questions or solve our puzzles, prior to or apart from that ever-open and daily-renewed committal to him in faith, for which the Holy Spirit enables us, and in which he continually sustains us.

The argument of this chapter has not been offered as a conclusive proof that God has certainly not provided us with any organ of infallibility in this world, or with any inerrant texts, more or less self-explanatory, and needing no more than to be assimilated and applied. But it has been argued that to suppose this is to suppose something quite uncharacteristic of his known method of dealing with us through his Holy Spirit; and that such a supposition removes the authority both of Scripture and of other texts from the context in which they have been given to us: namely the context of the nature and life of the Church, in which alone any such texts make effective sense.

CHAPTER IV

INFALLIBILITY AND INERRANCY

It is sometimes supposed that, to be orthodox in belief, Christians must make use in some way of the concepts of infallibility and inerrancy: that they must attribute infallibility in some conditions to the Bible, the Church, or the Pope, and inerrancy to some ecclesiastical formulae or to the text of Scripture; and that it is a mark of an unacceptable liberalism to refuse to make any such application. The argument of this chapter will be that both concepts are either valueless or else inapplicable except to God himself.

For the purpose of the argument, the term 'infallible' will be taken to mean exempt from all liability to be deceived, and will be used of persons and institutions; the term 'inerrant' will be taken to mean free from all error, and will be used of verbal matter. In current usage both terms can carry both meanings: thus the *Oxford English Dictionary,* s.v. 'infallible,' gives two main senses of the word, the first of which is the one which we shall use. The senses are (1) 'of persons, their judgments, etc. Not liable to be deceived or mistaken; incapable of erring.' (2) 'Of things. Not liable to fail, unfailing. (a) Not liable to prove false, erroneous, or mistaken; that unfailingly holds good.' A promise is given as an instance. (b) 'Not liable to fail in its action or operation.' A cure is given as an instance. (c) 'That cannot fail to be or come': e.g. a result. Correspondingly, the noun infallibility is given meanings: '1. The quality or fact of being infallible or exempt from liability to err; and 2. the quality of being unfailing, or not liable to fail; unfailing certainty.' 'Inerrant,' in the Dictionary, apart from an obsolete sense 'not wandering,' is given the meaning 'that does not err; free from error; unerring.' A creed is an instance of this. The noun 'inerrancy' is quoted of a book; but also of the Pope, and of our ancestors: a sense in which we shall prefer the word 'infallibility.'

It is common enough to hear Christians using the term 'infallible' of the Church, and 'inerrant' of the Bible; yet not much thought is needed to see that both concepts are of extreme difficulty and obscurity when applied to human comprehension or words about such high matters as God's revelation to mankind. That God himself is infallible is of course the belief of every theist, whether Christian or other; even though the late H. G. Wells apparently had his doubts about it. It follows of course that if a set of words can be attributed directly to God himself, they are inerrant words. Still, difficult and obscure as both concepts are, when applied to persons or to the Church, yet a discussion of the subject is certainly called for, since many Christians do so apply them, and attach importance to doing so.

There is indeed a possible application of the term 'infallible,' which is open to no objection, though it would be odd to use so dignified a word. It could be said, for instance, that a schoolboy was infallible in the lower reaches of the multiplication table, if he never made mistakes in it. And so with the term 'inerrant': a book of logarithmic tables might be called inerrant, if there were no mistakes in it, and no misprints. But the word would be odd in this application; we should be more likely to say 'perfectly accurate.' Similarly, it might, but probably would not, be said that the Table of Contents at the beginning of a printed Bible was inerrant, if it recorded with perfect accuracy the titles of the books, and the pages on which they began. But it is plainly not with any such application of either term that our discussion in this chapter is concerned.

Yet extremely odd things are often said on the subject, as if they had only to be expressed to be accepted by all Christians who mean to be orthodox and 'catholic.' Thus in the essay by A. H. Rees in a pamphlet called *The Infallibility of the Church* by H. Beevor and A. H. Rees (S.P.C.K., not dated, but about 1938), section 7, in italics, is headed 'The only alternative to belief in infallibility is individual opinion.' The argument there presented will hardly convince any one who is not predisposed to accept the conclusion; we certainly do not reason in this way on any other subject, even on the most difficult ones. No one would say in reference to historical, political, or ethical judgments that 'the only alternative to belief in infallibility is individual opinion.' The following sentence is a fair specimen of the sort of thing that is often said, but seems wholly false to those who are not inclined already to agree with the writer: 'Thus, we have seen that an infallible authority is *a priori* demanded by a revealed religion; that Christians have always either expressly believed in such an authority, or at least have acted on the assumption of such an authority. Where they have denied this, the denial of the fact of Revelation has followed' (p. 27). All three of the assertions in this sentence seem to be false.

We are not entitled to guess why this writer believed the assertions to be true; but it is easy to see why they may appear plausible to some people. God's revelation given to us in Jesus Christ is certainly final and complete; and it may appear to be likely that he has provided some organ on earth endowed with infallibility on the subject, and competent to put out inerrant words. But there is no reason at all *a priori* why a final and perfect revelation should need to be so expounded. If authority in matters of faith is the same thing as the obligation on Christians to conform themselves with the Church into which God has incorporated them at Holy Baptism, the loyal and committed Christian will not be looking for any such thing; at least not unless he is trying to limit the extent of his involvement in the life of the Church. He would find it convenient if he were in one of the positions referred to in Chapter Two (pp. 24–5 above); but then it is not at all certain that he can or ought to be satisfied in this way.

There are great difficulties attaching to the whole notion of ecclesiastical 'definitions,' whether about belief or about practice. It is an imprecise notion at the best, and it seems to be impossible to classify 'definitions' in degrees of finality. In *some* sense, no doubt, definitions exist and are authoritative: for instance, the Canon of Scripture has been defined, though at no particular time, and by no particular person or meeting; and even so, the position of the Apocrypha (the deutero-canonical books of the Old Testament) remains equivocal, except for Roman Catholics. But all the difficulties about the status of definitions are at their maximum if we introduce the notion of infallibility in the defining authority, and of inerrancy in the formulae which it puts out. Our immediate concern is with these two notions, and the inherent difficulties in the notion of 'definition' as such need not be further discussed.

Supposing, then, that some person or meeting is taken to be infallible, at least three major difficulties arise at once : (1) we are no farther on, unless we have independent means of knowing that we were ourselves infallible in our assumption that there is this infallibility attaching to the authority to which we attribute it. For it is certain that neither in the past nor at present has this assumption been at all universally made by Christians. This point has been magisterially dealt with by George Salmon in his classical book *The Infallibility of the Church* (Chapter Three). It is interesting to see how this difficulty is dealt with by the writer of the article 'Infallibility' in the Roman *Catholic Encyclopedia*. He says (Vol. VII, page 794) 'Once we come to believe in and rely upon authority we can afford to overlook the means by which we were brought to accept it, just as a man who has reached a solid standing place where he wishes to remain no longer relies on the frail ladder by which he mounted.' The fallacy is clear, since the question at issue is precisely whether you are on a solid standing ground or not. The 'ladder' has not become irrelevant. Psychologically, no doubt, the advice is often effective : 'You are on board the infallible ship ; go on reminding yourself that it is infallible. Of course there is nothing to worry about.' But rationally it is certainly a case for the application of a favourite aphorism of Fr. Herbert Kelly : 'Your reasoning is a part of the content of your conclusion.'

(2) The second thing needed if there is to be any value in having an infallible authority is an exact, indeed an infallible, knowledge of when the conditions for the exercise of infallibility have been met, or at least of what statements have been put out under such conditions, and are therefore inerrant. The view that the entire verbal contents of Scripture are inerrant will be considered in Chapter Seven of this book. More than one criterion has been proposed by which to tell which ecclesiastical pronouncements are to be held inerrant ; but they all demand a robust confidence that they are true criteria, and that they can be infallibly applied. Verbally, Roman Catholics were provided with a criterion of this kind by the Vatican Council of 1870 ; but as to the occasions on which it has been in fact applicable, there is no kind of agreement among them. More will be said about this at a later stage in this discussion.

(3) A third thing is also needed if any one besides the infallible authority itself is to get any profit from this wonderful gift: the infallible authority must be able to communicate to others the matter about which it is infallible, without any kind of loss or distortion. That is, first, words must be found adequate to express the matter; and then people must be found capable of assimilating it with complete correctness. The author of the article already quoted from the Roman *Catholic Encyclopedia* frankly admits that there is no guarantee that the last half of this condition will be fulfilled. He says (page 790) 'We mean . . . that the Church is infallible in her objective definitive teaching regarding faith and morals, not that believers are infallible in their subjective interpretation of her teaching. This is obvious in the case of individuals, any one of whom may err in his understanding of the Church's teaching.' We might add that if *any one* may err in this way, then so may *all* err. It is even harder to suppose that, on any major matter concerning the relationship of God himself with his world or with mankind, it is at all possible for any words to be found adequate to express it inerrantly, even if there is an infallible authority competent to understand it perfectly.

Thus the difficulties pile up on each other: can men, in any conditions, infallibly comprehend any major part of God's revelation, since infallible means exempt from *all* error and imperfection of understanding? If that is possible, then can any text expressed in ordinary human words be adequate to render the matter without distortion or loss? If human language can express this, then can people be found capable of assimilating without loss the meaning thus inerrantly expressed? Unless these three questions at least can be answered affirmatively, the whole concept of infallibility and of verbal inerrancy is of no use, but rather serves to mystify and confuse.

There is indeed no need to argue, as cynics have often done, that to mystify and to confuse has commonly been in fact the purpose of maintaining a claim to infallibility. It is more likely that the claim has been founded on the odd argument that any real revelation from God must *a priori* be expressed by an authority exempt from deception of any kind in words exempt from inadequacy of any kind. This inference is not fairly to be rebutted by the parallel, which in one way or another impressed John Wyclif and the late Professor H. L. Goudge (see *The Church of England and Reunion,* S.P.C.K., 1938), that infallibility and impeccability stand or fall together, and therefore that if we have not got the latter, we cannot have the former. There does not seem to be any cogent reason why these two things should be linked together in this way. But it may still appear to us that to assume the one is as gratuitous as to assume the other. We know for certain that there is no impeccability on earth, and we do not in the same way know that there is no infallibility; but the one may seem to be in itself as unlikely as the other. There would be a close correspondence between the two arguments: one would run 'Since our Lord came to do away with all sin, he must have left on earth some means by which it may be totally avoided,' and the other would run 'Since our Lord came to reveal total truth, he must have left on earth some means by which it may be taught without any admixture of error.'

It has so far been assumed in this discussion that the infallibilist is concerned to maintain both an infallible authority and an identifiable set of inerrant formulae put out by this authority in virtue of its infallibility. And this is in fact the form in which the claim has usually been made. But in theory the infallibility of the authority could be regarded as unimportant, and all the stress could be laid on the availability of inerrant formulae, whether the authority putting them out knew what they meant or not. This would be a kind of modern application of what was believed in classical Greece about the Delphic oracle: the priestess in a trance uttered sounds to the rational meaning of which she was indifferent, and the interpreters translated these sounds into intelligible sentences according to known rules, without having any inspiration of their own. The task of interpreting the Bible has sometimes been regarded very much according to this scheme.

Still, assuming the usual notion of an infallible authority, whose infallibility enables it on certain conditions (such that it can be certainly known when they are present) to put out inerrant formulae, it seems beyond doubt that at least these three things must concur if the infallibility and inerrancy are to be of any value: first, the subject dealt with must be one on which short statements can be conceived to be exhaustively true, as opposed to merely being helpful or illuminating; secondly, the statements put out must be patient of only one correct interpretation, and so be free from all serious ambiguity; thirdly, the hearers or recipients must be capable of an adequate comprehension of the statements put out. The usefulness of infallibility and inerrancy is altogether dependent on its being quite certain, as opposed to merely probable, that all these three requirements are being met at the same time.

It has already been hinted, and the fact must now be strongly emphasized, that infallibility is in itself credible in direct proportion to the simplicity of the subject involved; so also is the credibility of there being inerrant statements to be had, and of there being capable recipients of such statements to be found. When a sufficiently simple subject is involved, we may believe that all three requirements can be met, though a careful scrutiny of each separately is always needed before we can be sure that they have all been met at once. But then the *need* for infallibility is proportioned directly to the obscurity or complexity of the subject; so that we are most likely to have it where we least need it, and vice versa.

Thus, infallibility is common enough, but not needed, in matters which any one in mental health can judge infallibly for himself, as in discrimination of primary colours, or of the common species of animals. In historical or political judgments, it is very much to be wished for, but we are very sure it is not to be had.

To all this, the infallibilist will say that the whole point has been neglected : namely that God has made a special miraculous provision of an infallible authority, of inerrant statements, or of both. His arguments to show that God has done this must necessarily be *a priori* ones. Some people find, and some people will probably continue to find, these arguments acceptable; and they join the ranks of the Church of Rome, or else of 'fundamentalist' Protestantism. With others, as with the writer of this book, these *a priori* arguments carry no conviction at all : it seems to them no evidence of faith in God, but rather of the very opposite, to say that God *must* have provided such an authority on earth, or such statements, if there is to be any firm assurance in our belief or definiteness in its contents.

D

The proper way to proceed in disputing such an *a priori* assumption as this is to argue *a posteriori* that God does not seem in fact to have provided these things. The method must be to look at the formulae supposed to be inerrant. If this inspection shows either of two things : either that some of them do contain demonstrable error, or that the claim is in fact now only maintained in respect of statements of so transcendental a kind that no inspection could show anything about their truth or falsity, then the *a priori* assumption will be so far discredited. The general conclusion to which the present argument is meant to lead is that the former of these two things results from looking at the words of Scripture : they do contain demonstrable error ; and that the latter is the case with those statements to which modern Roman Catholics agree in attributing inerrancy : they include no statements on whose truth any inspection could throw any light at all. Leaving Scripture to be discussed in Chapter Seven, a few words may now be said about infallibility as it is now maintained by those Roman Catholics whose work commands general respect.

It is no part at all of the aim if this book to make a case against Roman Catholic beliefs : indeed, the line they take about infallibility seems to be wiser and more convincing than any other line would be—provided you have to admit the concept at all. There is no temptation at all to exaggeration or parody in discussing the current Roman view of infallibility. But it will be advisable to quote a short description of what this is ; and for this purpose the following sentence from the book on *Roman Catholicism* by Fr. Thomas Corbishley in Hutchinson's University Library (no. 51, 1950) will serve well enough : 'It is a strictly limited gift, involving nothing more than the claim that when the Pope, speaking officially as Christ's representative on some question of faith or moral principle, makes some pronouncement to be accepted by the whole Church, he is safeguarded by the Holy Spirit from making a mistake' (op. cit., p. 125).

There is often a danger in discussions on this subject, that one's interlocutor turns out to be using the word simply as an imposing synonym for being habitually in the right. This danger does not arise in talking with informed Roman Catholics : as the writer of the article previously quoted from the Roman *Catholic Encyclopedia* says (p. 790) 'infallibility means more than exemption from actual error; it means exemption from the possibility of error.' This is very important, especially in making any kind of review of what has been officially taught on the subject by Roman Catholicism in periods earlier than the nineteenth century.

It is notoriously rash to try to prove a negative conclusion on such a matter as this, but it is at least very difficult indeed to find any clear official teaching earlier than that century which affirms infallibility, as distinct from assertions that the Pope is always right in what he says. Mediaeval popes were just like many other people in positions of authority in being very much given to asserting that they were always right. Both the word and the concept were no doubt common matters of controversial discussion after the period of the Reformation : Archbishop Laud's controversy with Fisher the Jesuit is largely concerned with it. But they are remarkably seldom to be found at all before the controversies of the sixteenth century : Lewis and Short quote the adverb as occurring once in St. Augustine, but the very full index to the eleven-volume Gaume edition of his works has no entry on the subject. Nor does the word get any entry in the standard dictionary of late Latin, du Fresne's (du Cange's) *Glossarium*. As for its place in official statements from Rome, a fairly careful search of Denzinger's *Enchiridion* gives the following results.

None of the texts referred to in Denzinger's index seems to contain either the word or the concept at any earlier time than 1690. What they all seem to say, in one way or another, is that Rome has the right to define authoritatively on questions of faith or morals, and thereby to close those questions.

There seems to be nothing at all about infallibility in the decrees of the Council of Trent, at least as Denzinger records them : nor was there in the famous 'Creed' of Pius IV, of which very much practical use has since been made, until a phrase was inserted in it in 1877 (a significant date) about 'the primacy and infallible "magisterium" of the Roman Pontiff.' The only occurrence of the word which a fairly careful search has revealed in Denzinger's texts before the nineteenth century is one in a list of the Jansenist errors condemned by Alexander VIII in 1690. This runs 'the assertion of the Roman Pontiff's authority over an œcumenical Council, and of his infallibility in deciding questions of faith, is a vain one, many times refuted.'

It is only when you get to the reign of Pius IX (1846–78) that the idea and the word begin to come regularly in official documents issued from Rome. Yet it remains rare until the Vatican Council itself (1869–70), in and after which it is common enough. It is by no means confined there to the famous and crucial words put out at the fourth session of the Council on July 18th, 1870. These words occur in Chapter 4 ('On the infallible *magisterium* of the Roman Pontiff') of the *Dogmatic Constitution I concerning the Church of Christ*. The crucial section of the chapter reads as follows:

'We therefore, adhering faithfully to the tradition received from the beginnings of the Christian faith, for the glory of God our Saviour, the exaltation of the Catholic religion and the salvation of the Christian peoples, do, with the approbation of this holy Council, teach and define that it is a divinely revealed dogma that the Roman Pontiff, when he speaks *ex cathedra*— that is, when acting as shepherd and teacher of all Christians, he, by his supreme apostolic authority, defines a doctrine touching faith or morals which is to be held by the whole Church— enjoys, by the divine assistance promised to him in Blessed Peter, that infallibility with which the Divine Redeemer willed that his Church should be endowed when defining a doctrine touching faith or morals; consequently such definitions by the Roman Pontiff are of themselves—not by the consent of the Church— irreformable.' The translation here given is the one used by the English Dominican Fathers in their English version of Cardinal Gasparri's *The Catholic Catechism* (Sheed and Ward, 1932).

What is very noticeable about this statement is the modesty of the claim, at least if it is interpreted according to the literal meaning of the words, in the way in which legal statutes are interpreted. Indeed, the words themselves are patient of the following interpretation, to which the writer of this book would happily subscribe; though no doubt it would be disingenuous to claim the right to accept it in this way. It could be pointed out that the only infallibility claimed is 'that . . . with which the

Divine Redeemer willed that his Church should be endowed,'
etc.; and this is verbally consistent with the view that he did
not will it to be endowed with any infallibility. Then, all that is
claimed, as far as the words go, for the definitions issued under
the specified conditions is that they are 'irreformable'; not even
that they are true, and certainly not that they are inerrant. These
remarks are not made with any controversial purpose at all; but
rather to point out how extremely reticent and modest the
Church of Rome is in her most crucial definition on this question. We can hardly expect this extreme reserve to be kept in
popular teaching, and in fact we do find the claim inflated and
extended in various ways.

The next question which an enquirer will want to ask is 'On
how many occasions is the Pope believed to have put out definitions which fulfil the required conditions?' To this question,
which is not very often explicitly raised in popular Roman
Catholic books, there is no agreed answer. Where the question
is not raised, the reader is left to assume that the strictly defining
words in any papal pronouncement to the whole (Roman Catholic) Church about a matter of faith or morals is put out under
this guarantee of infallibility. It is of course readily allowed that
this guarantee does not cover the rest of the pronouncement,
apart from the actual defining words, but we are left to infer
that it does cover at least some sentences in many hundreds of
papal pronouncements.

Dom Cuthbert Butler, near the end of his book on *The
Vatican Council* (2 vols., Longmans, 1930), includes a very careful and judicious discussion of the question how many papal
definitions may be regarded as covered by the definition of infallibility in the Vatican decree. He is also careful to estimate
what kind of adherence Roman Catholics give to such formal
definitions as are not covered by it.

Thus, on page 226 of the second volume, we read 'The
writers we have being using, Choupin and Dublanchy, point out
that adherence to such teaching not infallible is not the firm
assent of faith, but a prudent assent based on a moral conviction
that such teaching will be right.' 'Choupin (p. 85) lays down:
"Whereas an infallible *ex cathedra* definition is absolutely true,
irreformable, unchangeable, and to be accepted with an abso-

lute certitude and a full and entire submission; a doctrinal
decision of the supreme teaching authority, not guaranteed by
the charisma of infallibility, is to be accepted by a judgment that
it is prudent and sure to regard this proposition as true—and
this with an interior intellectual adhesion, though such adhesion
be not a definitive absolute judgment, irreformable of itself".'

A little later, on pages 227 and following, Dom Butler con-
tinues 'Nowadays Catholics . . . are prepared to accept as right
and true a great body of teachings and judgments of the Popes,
without requiring to know that it is guaranteed infallible, trusting to the providence of God over the teaching authority of the
Church . . . '

'Dublanchy in the *Dictionnaire*' (that is, the *Dictionnaire de
Théologie catholique*) 'gives a list of papal as distinct from con-
ciliar utterances which by common consent are looked upon as
certainly infallible *ex cathedra* definitions according to the
Vatican decree. There are just twelve such in the whole range
of Church history: six are positive statements of catholic doctrine, beginning with the Tome of St. Leo, ending with the
definition of the Immaculate Conception by Pius IX; six are
condemnations of erroneous propositions of Luther, Jansenius,
Molinos, Fénelon, Quesnel, Council of Pistoia. The "Quanta
Cura" of Pius IX, 1864, is left doubtful; the "Mirari Vos" of
Gregory XVI . . . is not in the list—its *ex cathedra* character
was one of Ward's chief theses. As for the Syllabus of 1864, very
commonly defended as *ex cathedra* by the theologians of the
sixties and seventies . . . , its infallibility is dismissed as now
almost given up: "A peuprès abandonnée".'

The first paragraph we quoted from Dom Butler provides,
perhaps, a sufficient answer to the very obvious objection that it
must be puzzling to have a definition of infallibility without
knowing what definitions it covers; though many people who
are not Roman Catholics will probably still feel there is some
artificiality about that situation. If they go on to wonder why
the list is so short, they may guess that the answer is that if you
make it any longer, it becomes hard to find any principle on
which to exclude some formal definitions addressed to the whole
Church about faith or morals which have in fact been shown to
be erroneous. A well-known instance of this is the decree of

Eugenius IV 'pro Armenis' of 1439, in which the Pope defines the 'matter' in the Sacrament of ordination to the priesthood as the giving of a chalice with wine and of a paten with bread. This is now agreed by all to be wrong, since for many centuries no such ceremony was observed in the Church at all.

It is certainly hard to see how a list of infallible definitions can be compiled by a Roman Catholic without any regard at all to mistaken definitions in the past. If none were known to have proved mistaken, presumably a much longer list would have been made : the actual words of the Vatican decree seem to justify a long list.

The general conclusion towards which the argument of this chapter ends is that the whole notion of an infallible authority on earth, which under specified conditions issues inerrant words, is a mistaken and unnecessary one. It is not needed as a support for a firm and definite Christian faith; it is not possible to attach any meaning to it which can stand up against rigorous criticism; and it is always in danger of degrading faith into a cowardly passivity. Something has already been said about the first two objections; a later chapter will deal with the third, under the heading of Idolatry.

CHAPTER V

TRUTH AND TRUTHS

So much has already been said in this book, especially in the preceding chapter, about the necessary inadequacy of any conceivable statements in human words to convey the truth about God's nature or his dealings with mankind, that the argument can hardly go any farther without some kind of a philosophical chapter about the relation of true verbal statements to the transcendent reality to which they refer. The subject is a difficult one; indeed, even the admission that this chapter will be a philosophical one may cause some readers to skip it, and others to look to see if it seems to be expressed in the fashionable jargon of the present philosophical generation. But there is no help for it: the subject may not be shirked, even if some will not read it, and others will dismiss its writer as hopelessly dated in his philosophy.

It has been said in the preceding chapter that the possibility of infallibility and inerrancy varies inversely with the depth and complexity of the subject concerned. It is common enough where it is not wanted, on subjects where almost any one may know all that there is to be known. It is not to be had, and, if it were, it could hardly even be said to *mean* anything, on subjects of a wide range and complexity. Thus, on large issues of historical or political judgment, we not only do not believe any one could be infallible, but the notion of his being so is intrinsically meaningless and absurd. If a statement on such a subject is to be called inerrant, it must be about some minor detail only.

Yet we all mean something by calling the statements in the Christian Creeds 'true'; and every Christian preacher says many things from the pulpit which may rightly be called true. How are we to express the relation between such true statements and 'the truth' of any such deep, wide, and transcendent subject as God's revelation of himself to mankind?

It is hard to define what we mean by calling a statement true without using some synonym of the word 'true'; but perhaps it is fair to say that we mean that what the statement expresses is in reasonably close agreement, or correspondence, with the reality to which it referred. There are well-known difficulties about such a 'correspondence theory' of truth, one of which is that it seems to imply that one can put the statements and the reality side by side for comparison, which is often not possible. This difficulty should be braved, and we should say that a statement can be known to be true only when either such a comparison is made, or else when the statement is vouched for to us by a guarantor on whom, in the matter concerned, we can completely rely.

At once a qualification is seen to be necessary: the meaning of calling a statement true, as well as the possibility of infallibility and inerrancy, varies with the complexity of the subject concerned. Thus, such a statement as '2 + 2 = 4' is true in an unqualified way, because the subject concerned is abstract, and has no meaning or reference beyond the simple and completely defined terms used. When this simplicity is absent, no statement can be called true in this unqualified way; and there are many different ways in which it can be said to be true. It may be true on the whole, or for the most part, as if we say 'Germans are sentimental people.' Or it may be true, but refer to a trivial or unimportant feature of the subject referred to, as if we say 'Dogs sweat through their tongues.' There is a large number of relations which may hold between a true statement and the whole truth concerning the subject of the statement. What is quite clear is that merely to call a statement true does not tell you much about its relation to its subject, unless the subject is a very simple one.

*It is not nowadays usual, but it is most illuminating, to say that the truth of statements is *dependent* or *derived* truth, and that what it depends on or derives from is the reality of the thing referred to; statements are true or false simply in virtue of their relation to things or facts. This is so whether these things or facts are in the natural material world or in some other, as for instance a fictional world, or a conceptual one; that is to say, it

---

* In what follows, I am very much indebted to the late Fr. Herbert Kelly, s.s.m. Much of it is only a rewriting of a paper he read and approved in 1938.

holds of 'Barkis is willin',' or of 'Deism is a discredited theory,' as well as of 'Water freezes at 32 degrees Fahrenheit.'

Moreover, when the subject is not a very simple one, the statement, as it is made by any one, depends on its subject at two removes: directly on the concept or notion held by the assertor, and only mediately on the thing or fact itself. To cut out this intermediate step, one would have to assume that the notion or concept in accordance with which the statement was made contained the truth, the whole truth, and nothing but the truth about the subject, the thing or fact. A good type of case to illustrate this is what John Stuart Mill called 'real kinds' (*System of Logic*, Book I, Chapter VII, Section 4), that is 'classes, the things contained in which differ from other things . . . in more (particulars) than can be numbered, more even than we need ever expect to know.' The instance of a real kind proposed for consideration here is 'cats.'

When we make statements about cats, we make them, often at least, on the basis of much less than all we know about cats, which itself is a very small selection of all that is to be known about cats. At the issuing or generating end of this series is the indefinitely full and complex nature of cats as they are in real life; next below this is all that may be known about cats; then what we know; then the working notion or concept on the basis of which we normally make statements about cats; lastly, what is in fact expressed by any actual single statement made about cats. On this line of thought, we shall be inclined, in spite of its not being normal usage, to say that *the truth* about a real kind is the whole kind itself, its reality conceived as an object of knowledge; perhaps more accurately, thought of as potentially known. It may be nearer to common usage, but it is most misleading, to say 'there is no truth except in and through statements affirming or denying something.'

Even so, common usage also supports the view being commended here: it would be normal enough to say 'all that he says about cats is true, but he is a long way from having grasped the full truth about them.' In such a statement, 'the full truth' would mean the total nature of cats, thought of as potentially a matter for human knowledge.

John Stuart Mill, in the section of his *System of Logic* quoted above, contrasts with 'real kinds' classes distinguished from everything else *only* by one quality and such other characteristics as are necessarily connected with that quality. An instance would be the class of red things : all that this class has in common is redness, and such other characteristics as are plainly involved in being red, for example a reputedly irritating effect on bulls, a high absorption of light, an aptitude to be taken as politically symbolic, and so on. When we speak of the truth of statements made about such one-quality classes, we have little need to attend to the intervention of the assertor's notion or concept; it is, except in colour-blind people, in sufficient accord with the reality referred to. We know, nearly enough, all about redness, as we certainly do not know all about cats.

So far we have been thinking about our knowledge of, and our statements about, classes of things, and have pointed out that what we mean by calling statements true must vary with how much there is to be known about this or that class of things. But in order to consider how all this discussion of truth and truths bears on verbal texts concerning God's revelation of himself to mankind, it will also be important to think what is implied and involved in calling statements true when they concern facts or events in history.

This case is in important respects different from the case of statements about the nature of things as instances of a class. The difference of the two cases makes it necessary to refer to a distinction sometimes drawn between the meaning of a statement in itself, and the meaning intended by some person asserting it. The former is in fact a pure figment: words by themselves do not mean anything. Apart from someone's asserting them, they are no more than marks on paper, if written, or noises in the air, if spoken.

The meaning of any statement is what an actual assertor of it means when he asserts it; or at most what a perfectly qualified assertor of it would mean if he asserted it. It is easy to raise sophistical difficulties about this, as for instance by asking what is the meaning of a statement in Chinese made by someone ignorant of that language when no one is listening to him. The answer is that this would not be a statement at all. There remains simply the difference between what this or that actual person means by making this or that assertion, and what the ideally qualified assertor of it would mean if he asserted it. This difference is sometimes important, and its importance is specially apt to strike us in respect of statements about events in history; rather less so in respect of statements about things or classes of things.

Such a statement about an event as 'Napoleon sailed for St. Helena in the *Bellerophon*' is certainly true, but its meaning can be no more than what its assertor or its recipient can make sense of with his previous knowledge of the person, the place, the navy, and the historical context into which the assertor is fitting them. In every case the reference is *through* someone's notions or concepts *to* objective reality; and in every case it is wrong to identify our knowledge with the content of any number of statements we may make, unless indeed the subject is so abstract (as a simple arithmetical statement is) that there is no more to be known about it than can be quickly stated. In every case, the meaning of the statements refers beyond the assertor's mind to the objective reality; equally in every case what is in fact asserted depends immediately on the notion or concept in the assertor's mind, and this itself depends on the reality about which his knowledge is more or less fragmentary, according to how much there is to be known, and how much of this he in fact knows.

It is as much the case with statements about events as with statements about classes of things that the meaning of calling them true is by no means simple. We normally call them true if they correspond with fair accuracy to the event as it really is; the statement about Napoleon and St. Helena might equally well be called false, since in fact he went eventually in another ship, the *Northumberland*. This is just the kind of imprecision we often find in statements about events, and we shall find it when we consider the Bible in Chapter Seven. And even if there is no degree of inaccuracy in the words, the meaning they are capable of conveying will vary greatly according to the hearer's or reader's previous knowledge.

All the considerations hitherto mentioned in this chapter have some relevance to the kinds of statement contained in the verbal matter which is authoritative for Christians. At the very least they help to support the contention of the preceding chapter, that it is not only very hard to believe that on such subjects there can be any infallibility or inerrancy, but further that, if there were, the belief could have neither any precise meaning nor any practical usefulness.

There has been a large amount of theological debate in the last thirty or forty years about the medium of the Christian revelation; and in particular about how far the words in which it has been conveyed to us may be said to constitute the revelation itself, and how far that is to be confined to certain events, so that words can be no more than a record of the events which constitute the revelation. It is plain that there is here a large field for confusion and cross-purposes, since Christians of to-day can know nothing at all of the main revelatory events, such as our Lord's Cross and Resurrection, except through authoritative words in which the apostolic testimony to them has been handed down to us. It is too much to expect that a confusion which pervades almost every discussion of this subject can have been entirely avoided in this one; but some things at least appear to be beyond question. One is that until a few generations ago it was generally assumed that what was revealed by God to men about himself was primarily words; nowadays it is more usual to say that the revelation is of himself as he is, that this revelation is primarily given by significant events within the historical process, and that the words are not so much themselves revelation as the record of the revelation. This account is extremely generalized, and needs expansion; but it is easy to see that on the older view the concepts of infallibility in the human recorders and of inerrancy in the recorded words are much more likely to be made use of. On the more modern view it is easier to avoid them, and to say that the words, at least in the case of Scripture, convey a record of the revelation by use of many different kinds of literary expression: folk history, myth, lyric or didactic poems, and many others. All these literary *genres* mediate truth, and indeed do so more adequately than any merely literal language could; but the relation of the statements to 'the truth' is very various.

On the older view, the revealed words were taken as primarily a number of guaranteed statements about God, by reference to which we were to know what he is like. Our more intimate and personal knowledge of him was taken to be mediated through prayer, through inward convictions inspired by the Holy Spirit, and through direct encounter in Holy Communion.

With this last sentence a holder of the more modern view of revelation will fully agree; but he will begin by saying that the content of revelation is God himself as he is, that he reveals himself primarily by making known to us significant events in which he has acted within his world, and especially the series of events which constitute the Gospel, God's saving actions done through his incarnate Son Jesus Christ. It is then a matter for inspection to determine whether the record through which God has made known these events to us consists of inerrant words or not. We shall not want to assume that it must do so. The function of the record is to put us so far as possible in the position of those contemporaries of the Gospel events who had some right perception of their meaning. On the older view, our possession of revealed words puts us in many respects in a much better position than any contemporaries were in, since we know exactly and in so many words all that God meant to tell us about the Gospel.

Still, even on the modern view, there is need to evaluate the authority of the words by which alone we nowadays come to hear of the revelatory events. The first function of the Apostles was to bear witness as eye-witnesses of the Gospel events, our Lord's baptism, ministry, and teaching; his Cross and Resurrection; and his Ascension and mission of the Holy Ghost. But the apostolic witness in this form ceased as the Apostles died; it is recorded for us in the words of the New Testament, and to this the Church always points us.

More will have to be said in Chapter Seven about the 'truth' of these New Testament words. Meanwhile, they may be provisionally described in either of two ways: either as the verbal expression of what God enabled some contemporary or companion of a contemporary to assimilate concerning the events and their essential meaning, or else simply as 'true words' in the only sense in which words can be called true when they concern events of vast purport and implication, that is to say as conveying some knowledge about the reality with which they deal, but in a relation to it which cannot possibly be fully expressed.

The theological sense of the word revelation in what is here called the modern view corresponds closely to a perfectly familiar use of the word to describe our knowledge of other people. Fr. Kelly had a favourite example of this, which he used to call 'the lover's confession'; the lover is supposed to say 'Once I trod on her dress at a dance, by mistake; you should have seen the way she took it. It was a revelation.' This is a trivial but real parallel to the sense in which we say that the Cross of our Lord was a revelation. For us, the Gospel events constitute the revelation, which is always given by God, and is always essentially the revelation of himself as he is, in order that we may personally know him; and this is much more than revealing true statements about himself. But though the original eye-witnesses of the Gospel events did not receive the revelation through the medium of any words at all, we do so receive it.

Moreover, it is only partly true that the eye-witnesses received the revelation apart from words; for they needed to have some explanation given them of what the events signified. An event reveals nothing and nobody apart from some understanding of its significance. Our Lord gave his Apostles much instruction about the meaning of the Gospel events, both before his Passion and after his Resurrection. Our position differs from theirs in as much as we receive the testimony that the events occurred, as well as the interpretation of their meaning, through words. The application of all this to the biblical record is part of the subject to be discussed in the next chapter but one, and may now be left for that chapter.

What is to be firmly asserted at this point is, once more, that the relation between true statements which concern real kinds, individual persons, and still more God, and 'the truth' concerning them is never a simple relation, and is never capable of being accurately judged by anybody, however well informed he may be. Some instances of possible relations that may hold between true statements and 'the truth' were given earlier in this chapter: one was where the statement is true for the most part or on the whole, and another was where it is true but refers to an unimportant feature or aspect of its subject. And there is always the limitation that on such subjects statements cannot contribute very much towards a personal knowledge of the subjects they concern.

But when statements concern God and his dealings with us, there is a further large limitation to be made, which does not apply when they concern created persons and things. We are obliged to apply to God words whose meaning for us has been determined by their application to created persons and things. This is so with such statements as 'God is love' (1 John 4 : 8), 'The Lord repented of the evil which he thought to do to his people' (Exodus 32 : 14), or 'The wrath of God comes upon the sons of disobedience' (Ephesians 5 : 6). When we apply such terms as love, repentance, or wrath to God, we must be meaning to assert of him something *like* what we mean by asserting them of men, but with a large qualification which the addition of the phrase *mutatis mutandis* might express but not clarify.

It is well known that the subject of the 'analogous' character of all predications made about God is one which has a large place in any exposition of Thomist philosophy, and it is full of pitfalls for any one who does not normally think in Thomist terms. What Thomists say about it is not intended so much to prove that we can legitimately use ordinary language about God, as to elucidate the obvious fact that we always do, and always have. There is bound to be an opposition between two things : for on the one hand, the full and archetypal meaning of such words as love, mercy, and goodness, is what they have when applied to God ; human love, mercy, or goodness, is derivative and dependent on God's. Yet on the other hand their meaning as we understand it, and as it has formed our concepts, is what they mean as applied to creatures in this world.

Therefore, when Scripture or any other authoritative Christian text attributes qualities to God, we can only understand this attribution by reference to our normal meaning in applying such qualities to creatures, and by then saying that they apply to God only 'by analogy' ; and this is hardly more than a grand way of saying that they apply *mutatis mutandis,* while we remain ignorant in each case of what the *mutanda* are. The relevance of all this business here is that for us as recipients of a verbal record of God's revelation, the terms in which it is authoritatively expressed convey a *less* definite meaning than the same terms usually do, when applied to this world and to the creatures in it ; and even in that normal application, we have seen that the relation of what a statement expresses to the reality about which it is a statement may be of many kinds, and is often very far from clear.

A further but closely related point, which will also call for examination in Chapter Seven, is that poetic or pictorial language is often much more adequate for expressing what is true about God than literal or prosaic language would be. It is in no way a concession to fantasy to say that our Lord 'ascended into heaven,' and it is unlikely that educated people ever thought the phrase implied a local heaven up in the air, until the modern prejudice became fashionable that serious language about reality ought to be couched in prosaic and literal terms. The rise of this prejudice seems to be datable about the reign of Charles II, and is connected with the manifesto of the Royal Society, and with the names of Bishops Sprat and Wilkins. A good account of it may be found in Michael Roberts' *The Modern Mind* (Faber and Faber, 1937).

On subjects covered by natural science, no doubt we are right to prefer literal language; but there are many subjects besides God's revelation of himself where it may be of very little use, notably in descriptions of people's character and of remarkable actions: that is, precisely the subjects which are most analogous to God's recorded revelation of what he is like, and of his mighty actions. It is when statements can be exact and definitive that literal language is in place; where they cannot, more can be conveyed by pictorial or poetic language. The very rich content of many of the Gospel parables provides a good instance of this fact. Our Lord's account of the judgment, recorded for us in the last section of the twenty-fifth chapter of St. Matthew's Gospel, is not a parable, though one verse of it contains a comparison with a shepherd dividing sheep from goats. Nor on the other hand is it a literal programme for the procedure at the last judgment. It is direct teaching given in the kind of language most suitable for teaching on such a subject: vivid pictorial language, whose purpose is none the less not emotive but descriptive and informative. For describing a cosmic event which can only take place after the end of history, a literal and prosaic kind of language would be altogether inept.

It may be that this discussion has done nothing at all to

E

clarify the meaning of calling a statement true, when it concerns any subject of any concreteness, depth, or complexity. But at least it should have made it difficult to be content with a naïve and simple doctrine of inerrancy in the words of authoritative Christian texts, in Scripture, Creeds, ecclesiastical definitions, or anywhere else. Much, or even it may be all, in such texts can rightly be called true, as having a positive relation to 'the truth' of the subjects they concern, whether that is the nature of God himself, or his revelatory and saving actions. But it is altogether impossible to determine what this relation exactly is, or to make any complete or satisfactory classification of the relations of such statements to their subjects as they are in their total reality.

To say this is by no means to agree with the doctrine whose classical formulation was in H. L. Mansel's Bampton Lectures for 1858 (*The Limits of Religious Thought*); the doctrine, namely, that since God is infinite and absolute, no statements about him could be more than regulative truths, that is to say, indications given us by him of the ways in which he judged it right for us to think of him and behave in regard to him, but not necessarily in any positive relation at all to his real nature, which must presumably be wholly incomprehensible to us. On the contrary, we are affirming the positive relation of the statements to their subject, God and his actions. The statements do record the revelation given by God, which is revelation of himself as he really is. What we are saying is that nothing is being gained, or even really meant, by calling such statements inerrant.

Apart from the fact that the subject concerned makes it unmeaning to call the statements inerrant, there are other reasons too : in the case of Scripture, the great variety and range of the literary *genres* of which it consists is alone sufficient to make any unambiguous use of the term impossible. The barest kinds of historical information might intelligibly be called 'inerrant,' though any investigation of such statements in the text of the Bible makes it impossible to maintain that all of them actually are so. But it is hard to see what meaning could be found in calling, for instance, the Song of Solomon 'inerrant,' or indeed the Psalms themselves. As applied to the whole Bible indiscriminately, the word could have no consistent meaning at all; and it is wiser to avoid it altogether.

As applied to the words of, for instance, the three great Creeds of the Church, a meaning can be found in the term, but hardly a simple meaning, except perhaps in relation to such phrases as 'crucified, dead, and buried,' or 'suffered under Pontius Pilate.' The most that could be meant by applying it to such phrases as 'being of one substance with the Father,' or 'from thence he shall come to judge the quick and the dead' is that the words of the Creed are the best conceivable expression in human language of something to which no human language at all could be imagined as in any way adequate.

Perhaps the use of the term 'inerrant' of the Creeds is simply meant to safeguard the text from possible attempts to replace it by some other words which do not mean the same thing. But the use of ambiguous terms is not the best kind of safeguard for the text of the Creeds. It is more useful to point out that Christians accept the Creeds as classical and definitive statements about God's final revelation of himself through Christ. Classical and definitive, because the revelation remains what it always was, and there is no prospect of finding better verbal expression for what the Creeds say. We may no doubt expand and explain what they say; indeed every generation of Christians is constantly doing this. Christians in fact receive and accept the words of the Creeds in just the same kind of way, and for just the same kind of reasons, as they receive and accept any other integral feature of the Church's life and practice, whether it has any single classical expression in words or not. The question of 'error' does not arise as a separate issue at all; any conscious attempt to alter an integral feature of the Church's life, belief, or practice would no doubt involve the introduction of error, since all that really and consistently belongs to it has been taught and maintained by the Holy Ghost, the Paraclete. Partial and temporary aberrations have been frequent; but these things can readily be seen for what they are, at least in every matter of serious consequence to the Church, though it no doubt remains possible to raise insoluble puzzles about details. Our Lord's method and manner of teaching certainly does not encourage us to suppose that his perfect revelation is one about whose details there should remain no insoluble puzzles. The next chapter after this will perhaps help to explain why some people are tempted to think there ought to be none.

Perhaps the main reason why it is still felt that, after all, God's final revelation of himself to mankind ought to involve inerrant words somewhere, is that it is still taken almost unconsciously for granted that the revelation must primarily be a revelation of words. It is the aim of this book to argue that, though it is difficult to avoid this assumption, it is none the less a wrong assumption, and that to abandon it is to make no capitulation at all to vagueness or imprecision of Christian doctrinal belief; at least so long as we *do* make the assumption that the Church's belief has been guided and controlled by the gift of the Holy Ghost, the Paraclete, according to our Lord's explicit promise.

CHAPTER VI

IDOLATRY

THE word Idolatry at the head of this chapter has a rather portentous look, and seems to hint that some strong and specific accusations are to be attempted. This is not the case : the word is used to point a warning about a kind of temptation which has a perennial attractiveness in matters of religious belief and practice. Our discussion of it need not extend to any great length, and most of it can be kept at a general level; if the description is accepted as a true one, its warning can be kept in mind, and applied wherever, and in so far as, it is found to be relevant. The Bible itself supplies such specific instances of what is meant that detailed examples of it in modern times need not be given.

We are accustomed to many widely differing descriptions of the essential nature of idolatry; the one which will be used in what follows is that it means, more than anything else, the clinging to some smaller, more amenable, and more manageable substitute for the alarming and intractible God of genuine faith. This short description is plainly in need of expansion and clarification; it has received this lately in the book of Prof. H. D. Lewis entitled *Our Experience of God* (Allen and Unwin, 1959). For instance, on p. 89 Prof. Lewis says 'There is . . . a sense in which men . . . are apt to resist God, to be in conflict with Him or try to escape Him, *just because He is God*. But they will not do this in the first instance by merely forgetting or disregarding God. For they are also drawn to Him and need Him. They will thus try to limit or restrict their own consciousness of God by containing it within the media and symbols which are needed for its articulation. This seems to me the essence and beginning of idolatry.' Prof. Lewis works out his point in many other passages of his book, which may easily be found by reference to his Subject Index.

God's claims and demands on us are apt to be found too alarming and too unpredictable. We see that they call for intelligent initiative on our part, yet we do not know quite where we are with them. We may easily feel frightened, undecided, and helpless in face of them; and there are always those who offer us certainty, security, and deliverance from alarming responsibilities, at the price of submission to some authoritarian direction, whose credentials the temptation itself discourages us from examining at all critically.

It is plain that an attempt might be made to press this argument to discredit *all* definite authority in matters of religion and faith; indeed, that it has been and is sometimes used for that purpose. The criterion must always be found by an examination of the authority's credentials. But the *kind* of directions it gives may also be regarded: if they are unnecessary in themselves, and seem to owe their existence to their suitability as idols, then they are marked off clearly enough as different from the great permanent provisions which mark the life of the Catholic Church, such as the Bible, the Sacraments, the Apostolic Ministry, the Liturgy, or the Creeds. Any of these may indeed be abused in an idolatrous way, and some of them certainly have been so abused. But they exist for purposes very different from that: not at all in order to shield us from responsibility before God, or to settle for us what we ought to settle for ourselves. Rather the exact contrary: they involve us in responsibilities of a grave kind before God, of reverence, of intellectual labour, and of personal co-operation, often quite against our natural inclination. For it is characteristic of all idols that we do not have to equip ourselves by any effort, intellectual or moral, to receive what they offer, whether that is information, rules, or merely protection and the assurance that we are safe.

It may be that most error about Christian faith, both in past history and now, has something to do with the attraction of idolatry, in the sense of the word we are using. But the attraction seems to be stronger and more pervasive at some times and places than at others. Social historians have often described as more than usually prevalent at this or that time a sort of cowardly cosmic timidity. A classical instance of such a description is contained in Gilbert Murray's chapter called 'The Failure of Nerve,' the fourth of his *Five Stages of Greek Religion*. This is a description of the change of atmosphere after the time of his 'Stage III. The Great Schools of the Fourth Century B.C.'

It is only repeating what is being said all round us if we assert that, at the present time, totalitarian claims for an uncritical submission to an allegedly infallible guidance, backed by a promise to relieve us of personal responsibility, are more than usually acceptable to many people, both in politics and in religion. Such claims are said to be especially acceptable to young natural scientists at universities, but the constituency is a much wider one than that. There is no need to determine what are the main causal factors in this state of affairs : some people explain it in Freudian terms, others by reference to the atomic bomb, or to the impersonal anonymity of the modern urbanized herd. Whatever the causes are, the fact seems to be established. A wise priest, who has known the University of Oxford well for over forty years, said to the writer, 'When we were up, the difficulty was to get people to believe anything; now the difficulty is that they want to believe *anything.*' People in this uncritical mood are not apt to take much trouble in examining the claimant's credentials, or the rationality of his claim. If he is attractive, and offers security and freedom from unwelcome responsibility, intellectual or moral, the claim will be readily accepted. Many testimonies to this have recently been published from chaplains in universities, who have recorded their great difficulty in dealing with it.

In politics, this unhealthy wish to submit to a specious offer of security and freedom from responsibility is the background of the state described in George Orwell's novel *1984,* in which all the burdens are taken over by 'Big Brother,' and truth, conscience, courage, and many other virtues are no longer valued at all. The same sort of implications are also contained in the very different society described earlier in Aldous Huxley's satirical novel *Brave New World* (1932).

The Bible provides at least three notable accounts and denunciations of idolatry, which fit our, and Prof. Lewis's, description of what it essentially is. The clearest instance of all is perhaps that described in the account of Israel at Mount Sinai in the book of Exodus. God had appeared in majesty on the mountain, and the demands of his Covenant were revealed to the people, who then became frightened, and said to Moses (Big Brother) 'Speak thou with us, and we will hear : but let not God speak with us, lest we die. And Moses said unto the people, Fear not : for God is come to prove you, and that his fear may be before your faces, that ye sin not' (Exodus 20 : 19, 20). Moses' answer here is a profound one in relation to the whole problem of idolatry arising from cowardice and the reluctance to face responsibility : the remedy for a cowardly shrinking fear is a reverent trusting fear, and it may be that some thought about the two kinds of fear might help many people to-day who are involved in the problem of how to deal with fashionable idolatries.

Later, when Moses was not at hand, the direct demand for an idol in the crude form arose from the people : 'Up, make us gods, which shall go before us; for as for this Moses, the man that brought us up out of the land of Egypt, we wot not what is become of him.' Aaron made them a golden calf, and the people greeted it with religious enthusiasm : 'These be thy gods, O Israel, which brought thee up out of the land of Egypt' (Exodus 32 : 1–4). A scene of joyful religious observance naturally followed at once, and every one was happy.

This is the typical and persistent pattern of idolatry; first, a wish for refuge from the alarming nature and demands of the living God himself; then the call for a smaller and more amenable god as a substitute for the true one, and the enthusiastic and ostentatiously religious welcome of the substitute offered. The religious enthusiasm masks the fact that *faith*, in the sense it has as one of the three Theological Virtues, does not enter into the business at any stage. That is to say, there is no personal response of trusting obedience to a call from God, if that may be allowed as a short description of what St. Paul means by faith.

A second biblical instance of idolatry is detected and denounced in the seventh chapter of Jeremiah. The threat of the political power of Babylon frightened the people; they did not know what God was going to do, and they were disinclined to a trusting observance of his commandments. The prophet Jeremiah kept telling them that God would bring evil upon them, and that amendment of their ways was urgently called for. They therefore made an idol of the temple at Jerusalem, and the prophet is told to preach to them 'Thus saith the Lord of hosts, the God of Israel, Amend your ways and your doings, and I will cause you to dwell in this place. Trust ye not in lying words, saying,

The temple of the Lord, The temple of the Lord, The temple of the Lord, are these.' He shows how easily the living God can destroy any such hand-made idol, as he had done to its predecessor at Shiloh.

Idolatry of the temple is also a main feature in St. Stephen's speech recorded in the seventh chapter of the Acts of the Apostles. He shows how the divine promises to the House of God had in fact referred to his chosen people, the Church of Israel, but they had idolatrously transferred them to apply to a single building at Jerusalem.

A third instance is to hand in the ministry of our Lord, as recorded in the Gospels. The popular idol was the written Law of Scripture, meticulously interpreted and glossed. Of this idolatry our Lord says 'Ye search the scriptures, because ye think that in them ye have eternal life; and these are they which bear witness of me; and ye will not come to me, that ye may have life.' He shows here that the scriptures, by being made into an idol, failed to bear effectively the witness that God gave them to bear, and kept men from the Saviour they all referred to, when he was personally before their eyes. There may be some parallel to this at the present time: a too literalist attitude to the scriptures may well prevent people from hearing the voice of him to whom they witness. If so, the scriptures have become an efficient idol; for that is just what idols exist to do.

It is easy to see, even from the three cases of idolatry quoted here from the Bible, that the programme is not the same each time. At the foot of Mount Sinai there was a direct request for an idol, and an immediate conscious readiness to accept the idol offered. In the case from Jeremiah the prophet launches an accusation that the people have in fact made an idol of the temple; they would not be at all disposed to admit the fact; their idol was a talisman as well. In the case of the fenced and glossed Law in the time of our Lord's ministry, the position is a good deal more complicated: the Law had become an idol because the protecting fences and the glosses to make it apply to all situations in daily life had formed an opaque curtain which obscured the central meaning.

Modern appeals for idols, unlike that of the Israelites at Mount Sinai, never call explicitly for an idol, and idols are never offered for acceptance as such. In Christian or nominally Christian countries the invitation is, in effect, to 'receive *our* brand (in some sects very noticeably "our *exclusive* brand") of Christian faith as offering comfort and complete security because *we* (and not all those other kinds of Christians) have this great help to give you which the others have not got. So join our denomination, party, sect, or school of thought.'

It was said a page or two back that what is notably lacking in an idolater is *faith*. This is exactly the contrary of what is said by those who have idols to recommend. For, since the idol is an 'extra' that the others have not got, it can be represented as an act or a sign of faith to accept it; and it may be said that other Christians have not got faith '*in our sense*.' The solution is that faith is being used in two different senses: if faith means what it meant to St. Paul, unlimited trust in God himself, then the recourse to comforting idols is a mark of faithlessness. You do not really rely on God, and therefore accept an idol as offering that security for which you do not trust God himself.

Witchcraft has at some periods been a popular form of idolatry, but it does not quite fit the normal pattern; since it was another religion, not intended to help Christian faith, but resorted to as a side line, for short-term purposes, in order to give quick practical results. It was however sometimes in effect a substitute for Christian faith, resorted to because the latter could not be counted on for the results desired.

If reference may be made to some forms of idolatry which have beset Christians at times, no more is being asserted than that a belief has in fact been so abused; it is not implied that such beliefs have always involved idolatry. Thus at times the cry has been: 'Our Lord is the stern judge, implacable, infinite, and alarming. It is safer to have recourse to Mary, who is nearer to us, and more merciful; it is through her that all succour comes.' At other times: 'All God's demands on us are recorded in the written word of the Bible; put your trust in its literal text, and you can't go wrong.' Or again: 'There is (even "there *must* be") an infallible Vicar of Christ on earth; accept all he says, and you will be safe.' Since in ordinary English usage 'vicar of' means 'substitute for,' there is a possibility here of real idolatry. In fact, as has been pointed out by a modern scholar, the title is an exact rendering of the biblical word 'Antichrist,' which strictly means Christ's substitute, not his opponent.

When the issue is put baldly like this, it seems too clear to deceive any one; but of course it never is put in this way. The idol is recommended as a consoling help to keep us in the way of safety as good Christians; and so the danger to real faith may vary widely, according to the place given to the idolatrous extra. But our Lord's test is always in some way applicable: 'By their fruits ye shall know them.' The pride, arrogance, and lax moral principle of idolaters is always more or less perceptible. Charity and idolatry are not found to go together.

It was pointed out some pages back that *any* positive provision may be, and perhaps has been, perverted to idolatrous use. Indeed, it is hard to condemn anything in itself because it has been so used; and this applies certainly to the three things given above as instances. We may well ask our Lady for her prayers to help us; Christ's ministers on earth do certainly in some sense 'represent' him; and it is important to take the text of the Bible seriously, with detailed attention to what it says.

But within the Church in which God has placed us he has appointed, not indeed limited, safe, or foolproof substitutes for himself, but permanent signs and witnesses to his own presence with us, his operation in and for us, and his demands on us for our allegiance. These signs and witnesses of his actual existing Kingdom are just what idols are *not*; none of these signs is mechanical, safe, or foolproof; they are not short cuts to security, nor do they offer us limited liability or responsibility.

The main section of F. D. Maurice's great book *The Kingdom of Christ* is concerned to list and explain these signs and witnesses, which testify and articulate the full and unlimited claim on our allegiance to him who says now, as he said at Sinai, 'Thou shalt have none other gods but me.' These signs, according to Maurice's argument, are permanent defences against all idolatry, whether of written matter, of a vicarial ministry, or of mediators more accessible and less exacting than the One Mediator.

Maurice lists the signs as follows, and in this order: (i) Baptism; (ii) the Creeds; (iii) forms of worship (liturgies); (iv) the Eucharist; (v) the Ministry (so long as it is representative and not vicarial); (vi) the Scriptures, which interpret the other signs of the Kingdom, as well as being themselves one of the signs. There is no need here to repeat any of his argument to show how all these provisions are designed to defend us against idolatry. The chief thing is that they are appointed by God himself; they are permanent marks of the Church's life and practice at all times; and it is as such, and not as devices which may be resorted to by those who want special security from God's demands, that they are given to us. Neither Maurice himself, nor any one else who has read any Church history, would claim that any of these 'signs of the Kingdom' had never been abused as idols.

This chapter has not been working up to any kind of climax; the only suitable one would be an appeal that we should examine ourselves on this matter. A reference might have been made to useful treatments of the subject, such as we find in the chapter in Joy Davidman's well-known book *Smoke on the Mountain*, which is called 'Gods made with hands.' But this would be outside the scheme of the main argument, which is to discuss the place of authoritative words in Christian faith. The only reason for including the subject of idolatry is that the permanent temptation to it may well bias people towards a too literalist view of scripture, or towards making confident lists of 'inerrant' doctrinal formulae, in accordance with some *a priori* criterion which, apart from this bias, would not seem very convincing. When we are considering, in the two chapters which follow this one, how actual authoritative texts have been regarded by Christians, it will be useful to keep in mind what has been here said in a general way about idolatry in some of its commonest forms.

However prosaic our purpose in this discussion, we may remember that the New Testament itself contains the perfect treatment of this theme in the Epistle to the Hebrews. That epistle is addressed to Christians who were in danger of falling to the temptation to idolatry, from fear of the word of the living God. It is an instruction, a warning, and an encouragement to those so tempted. For instruction, the finality and perfection of our Lord's saving work is explained, and the impossibility of its being otherwise supplemented. For warning, they are told that God's word cannot be evaded : 'For the word of God is quick, and

powerful, and sharper than any two-edged sword, piercing even
to the dividing asunder of soul and spirit, and of the joints and
marrow, and is a discerner of the thoughts and intents of the
heart. Neither is there any creature that is not manifest in his
sight: but all things are naked and opened unto the eyes of him
with whom we have to do.' For encouragement, they are told
repeatedly that our Lord *has* delivered us from the fear which
tempts to idolatry. His saving work is described so as to lead to
this inference, which is drawn again and again from the argument: 'Seeing then that we have a great high priest, that is
passed into the heavens, Jesus the Son of God, let us hold fast
our profession. For we have not a high priest which cannot be
touched with the feeling of our infirmities; but was in all points
tempted like as we are, yet without sin. Let us therefore come
boldly unto the throne of grace, that we may obtain mercy, and
find grace to help in time of need' (Heb. 4: 11–16).

CHAPTER VII

HOLY SCRIPTURE

THE purpose of this book is to examine the function of authoritative verbal matter in a Christian's faith; and it is very clear that Holy Scripture is the largest corpus of such verbal matter. It is also much more complicated, and raises more difficult questions, than any other verbal matter with which our subject is concerned, such as Creeds, the definitions of Councils, or the writings of important Christian authors. This chapter will therefore be unavoidably the longest in the book; it will also be the most obviously tentative, incomplete, and inconclusive. It will at least, if it does no more, point out the relevance of many topics for the reader to take into his consideration, and to think about.

THE CANON

There is no important disagreement among Christians about the contents of the body of literature which they call Holy Scripture, or the Bible. The only disagreement at all is about the status to be given to the books which we call the Old Testament Apocrypha, and these will be disregarded in the rest of this chapter. Roman Catholics attribute full scriptural, or canonical, status to all these books except 1(3) and 2(4) Esdras and the Prayer of Manasses; Anglicans and Lutherans assign them the status of a kind of secondary scripture; and most other Christians exclude them altogether.

If some kind of provisional definition of the notion of a Scripture is wanted, it may be said to mean a collection of literature which is regarded by any religious body as normative for its faith and religion, in a way that no other literature is. These books are supposed to have been in some way designated by God as determinative for instruction and guidance about himself. This general description would cover the Mohammedan view of the Koran, and the Hindu view of the Vedas and Upanishads, as well as the Jewish and Christian view of their scriptures. But this chapter has no further concern with any other scriptures than the Jewish and the Christian ones.

Both Jews and Christians regard a definite collection of books as scripture. Hence the term 'canon,' or standard, for the list of books so regarded, and for their contents. Using this term, we speak of such and such a book as included in, or excluded from, the Jewish or the Christian 'canon' of scripture. Our concern in this chapter will be to discuss what is meant, and what is not meant, to characterize the books which are called canonical, or contained in scripture. But first it may be well to say something, in very brief outline, about the process by which the ancient Jews came to accept their canonical books as being such, and Christians to adopt the Jewish canon as it stood, and also to append to it the canon of the New Testament.

To do this with any decent completeness would be a very long job, and involve much technical matter; so nothing like it will be attempted here. But a few things about both the historical process and about the motives involved may be stated in general terms.

The Jewish scriptural canon contains exactly the same books as our Old Testament (without the Apocrypha), but not in the order in which our English Bibles print them. It has three divisions: first, the Law, that is, Genesis to Deuteronomy just as we read them; second, the Prophets, divided into Former Prophets (Joshua, Judges, Samuel, and Kings) and Latter Prophets (Isaiah, Jeremiah, Ezekiel, and the Twelve minor prophets); third, the Writings (Psalms, Proverbs, Job; the five 'rolls': Canticles, Ruth, Lamentations, Ecclesiastes, and Esther; and the books of too late an origin to be grouped with the Prophets, Daniel, Ezra, Nehemiah, and Chronicles).

These three groups of books came to be accepted as scripture successively: the Law some time about the middle of the fourth century B.C., or a little earlier; the Prophets by about 200 B.C.; and the Writings not definitively until the end of the first century A.D., though few of them were seriously disputed in the time of our Lord's ministry. In the synagogue services there was a lesson read from the Law, and a lesson from the Prophets; and it seems to have been in distinction from these two parts of the scripture which were 'read' that the third part came to be called 'the Writings.'

The usual notion of the ancient Jewish canonical status of the books in our Old Testament Apocrypha is that these books were included in the more loosely defined canon of the Greek-speaking Jews of Egypt, but were never candidates for canonicity in Palestine. This notion is now discredited. In fact nearly all these books, perhaps all of them except Wisdom and 2 Maccabees, were written either in Hebrew or in Aramaic; and they seem to have been simply unsuccessful candidates for canonicity in Palestine. But this question has no bearing on our present purpose, and may be ignored.

The other immediately relevant question, on what grounds the exalted status of scripture came to be attributed to any of the three divisions of Jewish scripture, is one which perhaps cannot be answered fully or with certainty. No doubt it arose with regard to the Law first, and not at all with regard to either of the other two divisions until the Law had attained an agreed scriptural status. Perhaps the following considerations were among the determinative ones.

God was understood to have given his 'Law,' that is to say his 'teaching' or 'instruction' in verbal form: the core of this was the Ten Commandments, written with the finger of God on Mount Sinai, but wider and dependent instruction had been given as well; and the form of this which was traditional in the greater shrines of worship had been written down, at least by Samuel's time, if not even earlier. When a book containing a version of this instruction was found in the Temple at Jerusalem in the time of Josiah, about 621 B.C., it was apparently assumed that this book had a scriptural status (2 Kings 22). The book seems to have been some form of what we call the book of Deuteronomy, or of a large part of it. Deuteronomy itself records a command by Moses that 'all the words of this law' should be written on stones covered with plaster, and that the stones should be set up in the land of Canaan; and this order is later recorded as having been carried out by Joshua at the proper time and place (Joshua 8 : 30–5). Once it was understood that God's verbal instruction to Moses had been perpetuated in writing, the notion of accepting a transcript of this instruction as scripture was easily entertained.

The first division of the eventual Jewish scriptures, the five books of 'the Law,' was essentially a transcript of the Law as

given to Moses—indeed, a conflation of more than one transcript of it—combined with a historical narrative to give it a
context. When Ezra read 'the Law' to the people after their
return from exile, it is not clear whether much, or any, of the
narrative matter was included; but certainly within a generation or two of Ezra's time the first five books of the Bible existed
as a body of literature, and had attained what we should call
scriptural status.

If then the main reason for the Law's attaining scriptural
status was that it consisted essentially in a transcript of God's
words to Moses, it may be thought probable that the second
division, the Prophets, came to attain it for a similar reason. In
the case of the Latter Prophets (Isaiah, Jeremiah, Ezekiel, and
the twelve Minor Prophets) this seems intelligible enough: these
books were the record of God's words spoken to the several
prophets whose names gave the books their titles, and if they
also contained narrative and descriptive matter, so did the Law
contain narrative and descriptive matter to give a context to
what God had spoken to Moses. But the Former Prophets
(Joshua, Judges, Samuel, and Kings) are what we should call
primarily narrative books; they are not obviously a setting for
God's words to a series of prophets.

The accepted solution seems to be that these books were
regarded as in fact written by prophets to whom God had spoken
earlier than he had to the series of writing prophets from Amos
onwards, whose books constitute the Latter Prophets; and there
is good evidence in Jewish tradition for this view of the matter.
If it were not so, we should naturally suppose that the reason
was that these books are essentially a record of how God spoke
to a series of prophets after Moses: some of them actually prophets in the strict sense, such as Samuel, Nathan, Ahijah, Elijah,
and Elisha, and others who might be called prophets in a wider
sense, such as Joshua and the Judges. But apparently this is not
believed to have been the line adopted. Anyhow, the whole series
of Prophetic Books was generally accepted as a second division
of scripture by about 200 B.C., though we hear of some doubts
about the book of Ezekiel later than this.

But by that date there were other books too which could be
grouped in some sense with these two divisions, the Law and the

F

Prophets. This is clearly implied in the Prologue to the book of Ecclesiasticus, which was written in 132 B.C. to introduce a Greek translation of a work written by the translator's grandfather about seventy years earlier. This prologue contains three relevant phrases : 'the law and the prophets, and . . . the others that have followed in their steps,' 'the law and the prophets and the other books of our fathers,' and 'the law . . . and the prophecies and the rest of the books.' It is not possible to be sure what were the principles on which the varied books in this third division, the Writings, were accepted as canonical scripture ; and it would not help the progress of this chapter to discuss here the different reasons which may have been influential in the case of this or that book.

A very brief outline may be added about the Christian canon of scripture. The Christian Church from the first accepted the Jewish canon as its own scripture, and in New Testament times had no other. For some time it was the wider canon, including all those books in our Apocrypha which were in the current Greek version of the Old Testament known as the Septuagint; that is, all of them except 2 (4) Esdras and the Prayer of Manasseh. Thus this Greek canon came to be regarded as the Christian Old Testament, and the stricter Hebrew canon as the Jewish one. At any rate, nothing in the Jewish canon was ever excluded from the canon used by Christians.

It is not clear when the notion first began to be held that Christians possessed a second canon, to which the character belonging to Holy Scripture should be assigned. But something may be said about the principles on which Christian books came to be regarded as scripture, and about the dates by which our New Testament books were so accepted.

Among the principles involved, the following certainly had a place. Words of the Lord were plainly of full divine authority for Christians, and an authentic record of them could lack nothing that scripture could afford. The Holy Spirit had also spoken through Christian prophets in as full a sense as he ever had through those of the Old Testament. Indeed, this seems to have been the reason why no human author's name is mentioned for the Gospels, the Acts, or for some of the more general epistles such as Hebrews and the First Epistle of St. John. The books were the product of the spirit of prophecy in the Church, and a human author's name would be out of place. By contrast, the epistles of St. Paul and some other epistles were topical and personal, and hence the author's name is found in them. The Revelation of St. John appears to be an exception, for it bears the name of John, though its contents are explicitly prophetic; yet they are visions accorded to one distinct individual.

The two chief criteria which seem to have in practice determined the acceptance of books as canonical for the Church were, first, whether or not the book was customarily 'read' in the services of public worship, and secondly whether it was regarded as either the direct composition of an Apostle, or had the authority of some particular Apostle behind it. At the very least, its contents must be in full agreement with such Apostolic books. A book which was thought not to satisfy any of these tests had no chance of being accepted as canonical.

It is not possible to make definite statements about the dates when the various books of the New Testament can be said to have attained canonical status; but the following tentative account seems to square with what evidence there is on the subject.

By about A.D. 120 it is likely that the four Gospels existed as a collected group of books, and also some corpus of Epistles of St. Paul, whose exact contents cannot be known. These books were apparently 'read' in services of Christian worship, as it is likely that the First Epistles of St. Peter and St. John also were.

The first attempt at making a Christian scriptural 'canon' of which we hear was that of the heretic Marcion at Rome about A.D. 140. His canon was an edited version of St. Paul's epistles (excluding the Pastorals), and a version of St. Luke's gospel. Apparently it was largely in reply to this heretical effort that the Church began to be more definite about the orthodox canon; but we have little clear information about it until about the end of the third quarter of the century. By then it is clear that the four Gospels were scripture, as it is probable they had been for some decades already. So also were the Acts, as going with St. Luke's Gospel, a collection of epistles containing nearly all those in our Bibles, and in most places the book of Revelation. By the year 200 the only two books in our Bibles about which there was nothing like general agreement seem to be the Epistle of St. James and the Second Epistle of St. Peter; though the status of the Pastoral Epistles was questioned in some places, that of the Revelation in some places in the Eastern Church (because of Millenarianism), and that of Hebrews, Second and Third John, and Jude in the West.

The earliest important document which gives a list exactly agreeing with our canon is the 39th Festal Letter of St. Athanasius, which belongs to the year 367, and after this period disagreements about the few disputed books diminish, though some are still found in the West about the year 400, and in places in the East up to a hundred years later still. Thus the general picture is one of agreement about all but a very few books by the end of the second century, but of local and lingering doubts about these few for two or even three centuries after that date.

HAS A 'LITERALIST' VIEW BEEN TRADITIONAL?

The discussion of the canon of scripture which has occupied the last few pages has no more than an indirect bearing on the general aim of this chapter; but it seemed worth attempting, since it is always easy to ignore the whole subject, and to argue as if the whole body of scripture was given all at once as a whole and ready made, though presumably no one really thinks this was what happened. It is certainly not suggested that the gradual growth of the canon is itself any argument against a literalist or infallibilist view of the Bible, though it is true that modern literalists are inclined to maintain a simpler view of this growth than the majority of other scholars hold.

Modern 'conservative evangelicals,' as they like to call themselves, often try to persuade us that the kind of literalist view they recommend has been traditional everywhere, or almost everywhere, in the Christian Church until within about the last hundred and fifty years. If in fact this were the case, they would certainly be entitled to insist strongly on it as an argument in support of their view. But their plea, in anything like the simple form in which they commonly allege it, is quite unjustified; yet to the modern reader who is unfamiliar with any but modern ways of thinking, the conservative's case seems complete. He can easily quote statements from authoritative Christian writers of

many different centuries which read to us as if they were meant
to express just what modern literalists think about the inerrancy
of the Biblical text; and any one who replies that they do not
mean that may easily appear to be making some over-ingenious
distinction without a difference. But the question is really important, and in spite of the difficulty of discussing it adequately
without presenting debatable assessments of earlier ways of
thinking, something must be said about it.

The subject is one about which it is extremely difficult to converse intelligibly with Christians whose tradition leads them to
use different phraseology from one's own. Those who are concerned to exclude one false extreme are very likely to misunder-
stand those who are more afraid of its exact opposite, even
though they may in fact be maintaining almost the same thing
as each other. Perhaps the only method which is likely to be of
much use is personal discussion and dialogue, in a context of
prayer and opportunity for thinking in silence. But it may be in
some degree helpful to sort out some suppositions which may be
maintained or rebutted, or to which we may fear the other party
to the conversation is unjustifiably inclined to commit himself.

One such supposition is that the most factually literal interpretation of which the scriptural words are capable is to be preferred to any other. It would perhaps be hard to find this
supposition anywhere before about the end of the seventeenth
century. But it is not to be rebutted merely by pointing that out:
it might be a valuable new insight. Still, it has no claim to be
presented as an assumption made without question for centuries.

On the opposite side, there is a liberal assumption sometimes
made that the books of scripture are a more or less fortuitously
assembled collection, a kind of unedited anthology, of the reflections on religious subjects of a number of people who were in a
position to get notice taken of their writings; and that some of
these writings deserved perpetuation much more than others. On
this view, inspiration means that on the whole the writings
handed down as scripture show their authors rather above their
usual form. No amount of errors, whether of fact, of taste, or of
moral quality, need cause any difficulty or even surprise. The
wonder is that the general level is so high as it is.

These two suppositions have here been expressed in a rather

extreme form; but some Christians argue from a fear of something like the former of them, and others from a fear of something like the latter.

The phrase 'verbal inspiration' has for some time now had the multiple function of party slogan, irritant, camouflage, and red herring. It is quite unprofitable now for any other purpose than that of concealing thought. Since the Bible consists of words, any one who maintains that God in any sense inspired its contents must suppose he inspired the words. If the phrase is taken to express the belief that the words were dictated by God in a process which involved the suspension or supersession of the writers' normal consciousness, then it is a very inefficient phrase to express that belief. It will be well if we avoid all further use of the phrase, though we shall certainly be concerned with the belief referred to in the previous sentence.

Another highly ambiguous assertion which has been debated is that the scriptures 'contain no mistakes.' It is a perfectly useless thing to say, unless it is understood that 'mistake' here means factually inexact reportage. If that is the meaning, then it is true that some Christians assume it *a priori,* and others deny it after a careful inspection of the Biblical text itself. But many who deny it in this narrow sense would affirm it in a wider and more important sense, and say that scripture contains nothing but what God intended should be in it, and that it could not be improved by adding to, omitting, or altering anything that is in it as it is now. Those who take this view would commonly say also that, while scripture contains nothing but what God had guided its writers to see and to express, the growth of its canon was also guided by him, so that it contains all, and nothing else than, the writings by which it is his will to teach his people.

There is a similar range of ambiguity attaching to the statement that the Bible is 'the Word of God.' By some it is taken to mean that the *words* of the Bible are in some unqualified sense the *words* of God, and only the words of men in the sense that human beings wrote them down. Sometimes the phrase is used in order to make a parallel between scripture and the Incarnation of our Lord; and this parallel may be made out in many different ways, and even be used to suggest analogies between views of the relation between the divine and the human elements in scripture and views, orthodox and heretical, of the divine and the human in the person of the incarnate Christ. This procedure is most unhelpful and misleading, since the purposes of the two divine actions are quite different : scripture is not given in order to exalt and transform the nature of written script. A similar analogy has notoriously caused confusion in eucharistic theology, and for the same reason.

Many modern theologians prefer to say that the scripture is the means by which God mediates his Word to us, rather than to say that it *is* his Word. By this they mean that though in itself it is inert, and may easily be misunderstood or perverted, yet it is given as a permanent means which God wills to use to address his word to faithful people who read it devoutly under the guidance of the Holy Spirit, and as loyal members of Christ's Church. They may add that through scripture God also sometimes brings those who are not yet disciples to become so.

This way of putting the thing is perfectly true, and it is important to remember that this is just what does happen with the reading of scripture. But it may be that we ought still to assert that scripture *is* the Word of God, and not say it is only the means by which his Word may come to us ; for that is all that any words can be. Words are quite futile except so far as they operate as means by which their meaning is mediated to us. So scripture is the Word of God in the only important sense ; and there is no objection to calling it so unless we suppose it could be improved by alteration. So it will not be useful in our discussion to use this phrase 'the Word of God' to discriminate between differing views of scripture.

Apparently literalist statements in ancient Christian writers do not usually, or perhaps ever exactly, mean what we at first take them to mean. Thus, for example, when St. Augustine in his eighty-second Letter says 'to those books of the Scriptures only which are now called canonical I have learned to pay such respect and honour that I most firmly believe no author of them made any mistake in his writing,' historical factuality can hardly have been what he had chiefly in mind. It is more likely to have been the complete obedience of the writers to God's guidance, so that they do not insert any mistaken notions of their own.

It is true that the attitude of rabbinic Judaism to the Old

Testament does often look like modern literalism, though it is
not in fact quite the same thing; but we should never forget that
the main concern of the earliest Church was to assert that the
Jews had radically misread and misinterpreted those scriptures.
It is therefore extremely unlikely that the rabbinic methods and
attitudes would be simply taken over by the Church. The New
Testament way of interpreting the Old can only be confused
with the Jewish rabbinic way if taking it seriously has to involve
exact literalism, as we are nowadays often told that it has. We
should also remember that, until well after the Reformation of
the sixteenth century, the main concern is always about how
scripture is to be read and interpreted, not about how God
guided its authors in composing it, though this latter question is
raised occasionally.

Modern conservative evangelicals often speak as if our Lord
himself took something very like their own view of scripture, but
the evidence they give for saying so amounts to little more than
that he took scripture to be authoritative, and to have been given
by God. So does any one who is at all likely to read this book. In
any case, it will be worth referring shortly to the chief passages
in the Gospels which bear on the matter.

Our Lord speaks, or appears to speak, of Moses as the writer
of the Pentateuch (St. Matt. 19 : 8; St. Mark 12 : 26; St. Luke
16 : 29; St. John 5 : 45, 46; 7 : 19ff.), of David as the author
of Psalm 110 (St. Matt. 22 : 43, 45), and of Daniel as the prophet who wrote the book so entitled (St. Matt. 24 : 15). Yet the
inferences are certainly not all compelling : prescriptions of the
Law can be called Moses' without any implication about the
authorship of the books in which they are recorded, and such a
phrase as 'the book of Moses' no more implies ascription of
authorship than would 'the book of Samuel,' or than we could
be held responsible for a similar judgment if we quoted *Henry
VIII* or *Pericles* as 'Shakespeare.' Much the same holds of
quoting Psalm 110 as 'David,' or referring to the Abomination
of Desolation as 'spoken of by Daniel the prophet.' In St. John
10 : 35 our Lord is reported as having said in an argument based
on Psalm 82, 'and the scripture cannot be broken.' This may
mean simply that a Psalm will not contain an unjustifiable expression, and one does not need to be much of a literalist to

believe that. Finally, and most conspicuously, there are the words in St. Matt. 5 : 18, 'Verily I say to you, until heaven and earth pass away, one jot or one tittle shall by no means pass away from the Law, till all come to pass.'

Yet within a few verses of this last saying our Lord launches out on a series of drastic reinterpretations of this same Law : 'Ye have heard that it was said . . . but I say unto you.' Elsewhere he said that a command in the Law about divorce (Deut. 24 : 1) was given as a temporary rule 'with your hardheartedness in view' (St. Mark 10 : 5ff.). Again, it is specifically noted by St. Mark (7 : 19) that, by what he said about clean and unclean, our Lord did away with the whole distinction. And yet it is most emphatically and repeatedly made in the Law. It is clear that his 'attitude to the scriptures' cannot be properly described in any short formula. It is in fact not at all certain that he did share the beliefs of his contemporaries about the authorship of Old Testament books; but, supposing he did, the fact need disconcert nobody who really believes that 'it behoved him in all things to be made like unto his brethren.' A great scholar once said that only a Docetist (that is, one who believes our Lord's humanity to have been only apparently real) would mind if our Lord did think Psalm 110 was written by David.

Both within the New Testament and in the writings of the early Church Fathers, what literalism there was is very much counterbalanced by the freedom with which the words of scripture are interpreted allegorically, when the literal sense seemed less useful. The literal sense is not denied, but at least it is subordinated, where, for instance, St. Paul allegorises about Hagar and Mount Sinai (Gal. 4 : 24ff.), or where he says that the precept against muzzling a threshing ox refers primarily to human missionaries (1 Cor. 9 : 9, 10). In many of the Fathers, allegorical or at least very non-literal interpretation is carried to great lengths. Sometimes rather far-fetched moral applications of the Biblical text are taken to be its chief meaning; and this procedure is very characteristic of mediaeval preaching (see page 120, below).

In other respects, too, it cannot be said that any of the great Church Fathers were literalists in the way many modern conservatives are. Thus Irenaeus specifically denies the literal meaning of the story of the Fall in Genesis 3; Gregory of Nyssa says the opening chapters of Genesis are not historical; and St. John Chrysostom faces squarely the discrepancies in the Gospels. What seems to be new in modern literalism is a kind of rigidity in interpreting the Bible's words. J. K. S. Reid, from whose admirable book *The Authority of Scripture* (Methuen, 1957) I have borrowed the reference just given to three great Fathers, also quotes with approval a summary remark from Fr. A. G. Hebert's *The Authority of the Old Testament* (Faber and Faber, 1947), p. 98: 'the inerrancy of the Bible, as it is understood to-day, is a new doctrine, and the modern fundamentalist is asserting something that no previous age has understood in anything like the modern sense.' Fr. Hebert goes on in his next paragraph 'When divine Revelation has been understood in a materialistic way, and it has been argued that because the Bible is the word of God everything in it must be taken as "literally" true, the discovery that many things in it are not literally true leads to the inference that it is not the word of God; and without doubt this inference is very widely drawn to-day.'

Fr. Hebert's contention is both true and important; the trouble to the faith of some modern Christian people is most unfortunate, and a little understanding of the different way in which people once thought of truth could cure it. The pity is that many people to-day are so educated that they have never been able to acquire any historical imagination at all. In writers of the Patristic and mediaeval periods, we do not seem to come across those anxious efforts to explain factual discrepancies in the Bible with which books by modern literalists have made us very familiar.

It is true that now and again one comes across the Apollonian or Sibylline view of inspiration applied to scripture, or the human writer is compared to a plectrum in the hand of the divine musician, who uses it to play what music he likes. But such ideas are exceptional, and, when they do occur, are not brought in so much to assert literal factuality, but rather to say that the Bible contains just what God, in his providence, meant it to contain. And that puts a different appearance on the simile.

Neither Luther nor Calvin were literalists in the modern sense; indeed, Luther's view of scripture is too little intellectualized for the issue to arise. His point is that the Bible is *itself* authoritative (*sola scriptura*), and not just a tool in the power of the Church. The issues at stake are those of faith in God through Christ, and of personal religion. It was later Lutherans, writing after the 'scientific' revolution in the middle of the seventeenth century, who interpreted Luther and the Confession of Augsburg as implying exact factual inerrancy.

In Calvin there is certainly much which reads to us as asserting what modern literalists assert, but there is also much that is entirely incompatible with it. He does indeed use the metaphor of divine 'dictation,' but he insists repeatedly on the Bible's being not only the word of God, but also the word of men. He also lays great emphasis on its barrenness apart from the *ad hoc* illumination of the reader by the Holy Spirit. This is more like the instrumentalist view, familiar to modern students in the writings of Karl Barth. The locus of the Spirit's work is seen as the heart of the Christian reader rather than the text of the book; and this makes a great deal of difference. And a modern literalist would not readily find himself at ease with the principle that all scripture speaks of Christ, or that it is called scripture because and in so far as it does this. But this principle in one form or another is common to both Luther and Calvin.

It is also worth bearing in mind that New Testament writers often quote the Old Testament in what would nowadays be called a very loose or approximate way. They use now the Hebrew text turned into Greek, now the Greek of the Septuagint which often differs from the Hebrew in important details, and now a wording which has no close correspondence with either. The last class of quotations is sometimes accounted for by suggesting that the writers are adopting the version in a current 'testimony book'; if so, that is only shifting the question about verbal laxity in quotations. Words may be altered to fit the context in which the quotation is made, or the original Old Testament context may be markedly disregarded. Perhaps the only New Testament book in which the quotations from the Old Testament are always careful and exact is the Epistle to the Hebrews; but this book always quotes the Greek Septuagint version, and not the Hebrew original. Also no problem arises here about possibly over-literal exegesis, since the quotations are all dealt with convincingly.

ARE THERE FACTUAL DISCREPANCIES?

This is not a very profitable subject, and it would be a waste of
time to deal with it at length; but it would be odd to leave it
out altogether in a chapter which is concerned with the sense in
which the words of scripture are authoritative for us.

Any one who looks at scripture with the presuppositions of a
'conservative evangelical' in at all a fully developed form will be
in no way disconcerted by any apparent factual discrepancies
which can be found in the text of the Bible. And, on his presuppositions, he will no doubt be right to be unimpressed. He
may say that there is a mistranslation, or a textual error in the
now current version of the original Hebrew or Greek. At other
times he will say that the two passages between which there is a
discrepancy are not describing the same event, as they seem to
be doing, but two different events. Sometimes this explanation
looks, on the face of it, so very implausible that we are reminded
of what the Victorian zoologist, Philip Gosse, is believed to have
said about fossils in rocks: that they had been put like that to
test our faith. They seem to point to an enormously remote
origin, but in fact we know from the Bible that the world was
not created at all until 4004 B.C.

To any one who does not make the assumption that if the
Bible is or mediates God's word it must be factually inerrant in
details, the existence of some discrepancies causes no surprise at
all; rather it seems extraordinary how accurate the history is,
even in the record of remote periods, such as the description of
the culture of the patriarchs, from whose time we can hardly
suppose any relevant documentary remains survived until any
part of our book of Genesis was composed. The reason is, no
doubt, that folk memory was extremely tenacious and accurate,
but no question of strict inerrancy is raised by this fact.

It will be best to confine ourselves to a very few factual discrepancies, and to keep to trivial instances which concern matters of detail only. This will do for our present purpose, though
it would be more informative to notice how differently major
characters and institutions are regarded by different writers
within the Old Testament; this however would take up much
more space than ought to be given here to the subject of discrepancies at all.

The text itself is sometimes plainly corrupt: thus 1 Sam. 13 in the Hebrew text begins 'Saul was a year old when he began to reign,' although long before that time we have been told of him that 'from his shoulders and upward he was higher than any of the people,' and he was known as 'a mighty man of valour.' The accounts of Esau's wives are quite irreconcilable with each other; if one compares the three relevant texts, Genesis 26 : 34, 28 : 9, and 36 : 2, the similarities and the differences between them make it extremely implausible to refuse to see any factual mistake. A third instance is the question 'Who killed Goliath?' According to 1 Sam. 17, David did; but according to 2 Sam. 21 : 19 it was Elhanan the son of Jaare-oregim (and he is a bit of a mystery too: see 2 Sam. 23 : 24). The passage in Chronicles which is plainly parallel to the final paragraph in 2 Sam. 21 says it was a brother of Goliath called Lahmi whom Elhanan killed. All three passages make it quite clear that the same Goliath is meant, by saying in each case that the staff of his spear was like a weaver's beam. Again, only an *a priori* principle that there can be no factual errors can allow none to be seen here.

It would be very easy, but extremely tedious, to quote many more instances of this kind. The simplest way to find a crop of them is to compare passages in Chronicles with those that correspond to them in Samuel or Kings. One might begin by comparing 1 Chron. 18 : 4, 21 : 5, and 21 : 25 with 2 Sam. 8 : 4, 24 : 9, and 24 : 24 respectively; and go on with comparisons of 2 Chron. 8 : 2 with 1 Kings 9 : 12; of 2 Chron. 14 : 5 with 1 Kings 15 : 14; of 2 Chron. 17 : 6 with 1 Kings 22 : 43; and of 2 Chron. 22 : 9 with 2 Kings 9 : 27, 28. But no reader can possibly want any more of this kind of thing.

Another thing the literalist ought to make up his mind about is what version of the text is inerrant. Many old-fashioned Englishmen no doubt thought it was the Authorized Version of 1611, and Roman Catholics have at times supposed it to be the Vulgate Latin version of St. Jerome. Eastern Orthodox Christians show that they are not literalists in this sense by saying that the Septuagint Greek version is equally inspired with the Hebrew original of the Old Testament. But for the modern literalist there is a dilemma : he may wish to say that it is the original Hebrew or

Greek of the autographs which is inerrant; but no one supposes that we have access to an exact transcript of this. All our texts differ in details from each other, and if any one of them is in fact identical with the autographs, there is no means of telling which of them it is. If he chooses the alternative of saying that this or that version of the text is the inerrant one, he is faced with the task of justifying his choice; and it is hard to see how he is to do that.

It is also hard to see how the literalist can be much interested in the process by which this or that biblical book grew into its definitive form; he will no doubt allow that there was such a process, but the investigation of it will not for him be very informative. For the rest of us, however, it will appear to be of the greatest interest and importance to study the historical growth of each part of the biblical literature, so far as it may be known or reasonably conjectured. We shall expect to learn a great deal in this way about the permanent meaning of the final products; all available knowledge of how the books came to be as they are will seem to us as relevant to our understanding of them as we think the study of any nation's history is to our understanding of it as it is now. We are bound to think that the extreme literalist is likely greatly to undervalue the study of the books' growth, and that if he does so he is missing very much which God could teach him by that study.

REVELATION

Among the questions relevant to the subject of the present chapter, none is more central than the relation of the words of scripture to God's revelation; yet the question is one of extreme complication and difficulty, and the intrinsic difficulty of the subject is increased by changes of fashion in the way some of the key words are used, including the word revelation itself. The subject has been discussed in many wise modern books, and much that is of importance has been well said. But the reviewers of these books have always been able to point to one or more important considerations which the writers of them have neglected; usually also to some pervasive bias which has continually affected their argument. The present short discussion is not undertaken with any confidence of its being exempt from either

of these drawbacks. Indeed, its brevity and its avoidance of all
display of scholarship may well make it highly vulnerable in both
these respects. But it is better to face a task in full view of the
impossibility of its adequate performance than either to ignore
the difficulty or to make no attempt at all to deal with the subject. At least we begin with no illusions about the prospect of
any neat or conclusive answers.

God certainly reveals himself to us through the Bible: not
only through the Bible, but in some distinctive and important
way through it. The meaning of this universal Christian belief
has been the topic of much recent thought, discussion, and
literature. It is the fashion to say that until lately the revelation
was assumed to *consist in* the words of scripture; or, more
accurately, in God's communication of truths about himself in
verbal form. Against this assumption it is then said to be more
satisfactory to take the revelation itself to be the actions or events
in which God showed himself or made himself known; in this
case, the Bible must be called the inspired record of the revelation rather than itself the revelation. It is possible to regard the
difference as consisting mainly in a change of fashion in the use
of the word revelation; for on the older view no one doubted
that the revealed words told us authoritatively what God had
done and said for our salvation, and on the newer view it still
needs to be said that the *record* of the revelatory events is definitive and also authoritative.

But certainly the newer view eases the transition from the Old
to the New Testament. On the older view, something like this
would have had to be said: that God had revealed himself in
scripture to the ancient Jews through the words of the Old
Testament books as they were severally composed, and then
through the whole body of them, once they were collected
together. Then, that his final revelation of himself in Christ was
at first not mediated scripturally, but simply through the words
and deeds of our Lord on earth; then, that from about a generation after his Ascension onwards, the final revelation for all
future Christians was located in the New Testament scriptures,
as God caused its books to be written, and accepted as together
constituting a second part of the canon. Any such statement as
this sounds awkward and unsatisfactory, and has to omit much

that is of great importance: for instance the fact that our Lord himself during his ministry on earth interpreted his own Person and work in terms of Old Testament scripture, and that the Gospel was preached and commended primarily in the same terms from the day of Pentecost onwards, before any book of the New Testament was written.

We may well accept the modern fashion of locating the revelation itself rather in the events in which God specially showed himself than in the record of those actions of which scripture consists. But this change in the use of the word revelation does not solve any questions about the nature of the verbal record, though it probably gives less encouragement to an oracular or literalist view of it than the older use did. It will perhaps lead us to say something like this: that the whole history of mankind in relation to God is full of God's revealing acts, and that scripture is the authoritative record of those among such acts which have the closest relevance to the central series of them which extends from the Annunciation to Pentecost, either as preparation for it or as sequel to it.

But the question still remains, much as before, what kind or degree of inerrancy belongs to the verbal record of this series of revelatory events. God *may,* for all we can tell from this argument, have provided a literally inerrant record of his specially revelatory actions, or he may not have given the record this characteristic. Whether he has done so or not must be investigated *a posteriori* by looking at the text of the record; and an inspection of it suggests that he has not. It rather suggests that factual inerrancy is no more a part of what God has given us in scripture than is information about truths in astronomy, medicine, or physics which were not to be discovered till many centuries after the books of scripture were written. But this inference will not in any way make us the more disposed to doubt that scripture contains a divinely controlled record of just those revelatory events, those and no others, which God knew to be relevant and sufficient for all the future generations of his people to know for their health. The conclusion that there is no inerrancy in the words does not lead in any way to the conclusion that the matter recorded was selected at haphazard, or without God's guidance and control.

But the newer view brings forward another question which the older one was apt to leave dormant. We are now to see God's revelation sited primarily in a series of *events*. But much of scripture is not a record of events; it consists largely also of poetical reflection or of moral exhortation, which has indeed some reference to events, but has also a timeless quality. The Psalter, for instance, contains reflection on particular events, but that is not all it contains. Similarly the utterances of the prophets recorded in the books called after them are all, or almost all, related to events in history, but they convey a revelation of God himself beyond their historical reference. Though this consideration applies more to the Old Testament than to the New, it does apply in some degree also to the New.

It may be that this apparent distinction between scripture as it refers to historical events and scripture as it goes beyond that reference is of little importance, and that there is no sharp line to be drawn between recording events and making general comments more or less remotely related to events. Indeed, no event can be recorded as being important, unless some kind of explanation is given in more general terms of why the event is believed to be important. Since the Bible consists of literature of several different kinds, Christians ought to give much thought to understanding in what way each of these kinds contributes to God's revelation of himself through the Bible. This subject was simply treated a few years ago in an admirable book by R. P. C. Hanson and Brian Harvey called *The Loom of God* (Dublin, A.P.C.K., 1945; new edition, 1955), and it is not easy to find so satisfactory a treatment of it elsewhere in a small book.

Mere narrative of events can only exist by taking for granted a sufficient knowledge of context and background, as is done, for instance, in the balder kind of mediaeval chronicles. Since this is true, the question still remains one of lively interest how we are to conceive that God not only caused the best selection of revealing events to be recorded in scripture, but also controlled the recorded interpretation of their meaning and context. It is possible that some light may have been thrown by this discussion on the place of the human element in the composition of scripture, but certainly none of the major questions about God's control of its human writers has been in any sense solved.

G

One thing of which we may be certain is that the knowledge of God which is to be conveyed to his people through scripture is the knowledge which is acquaintance rather than the knowledge which is only information. But this distinction, again, is of very limited usefulness, for acquaintance involves information, and information is of great value in deepening acquaintance.

But on such a subject as personal revelation for acquaintance and information, there has to be in some degree inspired reception as well as an inspired message. Our response to all God's revelation of himself, through scripture as well as otherwise, is what is in scripture called Faith, which is at once a gift of God to man, and an attitude which by virtue of this gift can be maintained by man as he faces God. The best simple definition of faith in this sense known to the writer of this book is the answer to Question 86 in the Shorter Westminster Catechism (1648): 'Faith in Jesus Christ is a saving grace, whereby we receive and rest upon him alone for salvation, as he is offered to us in the gospel.'

The exercise of faith in the receiving of God's revelation of himself, in scripture or otherwise, necessarily involves elements both of assent and of commitment; and neither of these is valuable or rational without some degree of the other, though their precedence may vary to some extent with different parts of scripture. In our reception of the classical Creeds it is plain that the element of commitment has precedence over the element of assent, as it still more plainly did in the first scriptural confession of Christian faith 'Jesus is Lord' (1 Cor. 12 : 3 ; Rom. 10 : 9). What first forced up the element of assent was probably the confrontation with denial and heresy. It remains important that we should keep the two in proper balance in any response of faith to God's revelation; and of this proper balance it might be difficult to find a better instance than the so-called Athanasian Creed, though at present it seems to be beset by many academic enemies. The question of Creeds may be left for the present, as it forms part of the subject of the chapter which follows this one.

It may be useful at this point to attempt some sort of provisional statement of the relation of scripture to God's revelation of himself through it, though it will have to be a general and a tentative statement. We shall say that the chief locus of the revelation itself is in the long series of historical events in which God acted, more than he did elsewhere, for the salvation of mankind. The central events of this series are the Gospel events from the Annunciation to the Ascension and Pentecost. It is in virtue of their relation to these Gospel events that earlier and later actions of God are recorded in scripture: either as preparatory to them (e.g. the call of Abraham, Moses and the Exodus, David and the Kingdom, the prophets, the first and second Temple, and any number of less vital ones too), or as consequent upon them (e.g. the work of the Apostles and others in spreading the Gospel after Pentecost). By extending this principle it may be rationally maintained that scripture contains nothing at all which is irrelevant to this historically conditioned revelation. It used sometimes to be a habit among theological modernists to depreciate the genealogies which occur in both Testaments; but such shafts were very ill-aimed, since it is a constant feature of God's way of dealing with us for our salvation to work by calling individuals and families to special tasks, to be in a special way recipients of revelation, and in a special way his servants and his messengers. Genealogies, particularly among the kings and the priests of his people in the Old Testament period, are closely relevant to the main theme.

The principle seems to be that in God's providence the canon of scripture records those events which he meant to be permanently on record for his people, so that they should know him by knowing how he had acted for them; that besides the record of the events, it should display enough of the historical and cultural context of the events to make them intelligible, and to show their relation to the climactic series which we call, *par excellence*, the Gospel events; thirdly, that it should also display the amount and kind of comment on God's actions and methods with his people, and about God himself as he had made himself known to them, which should serve as permanent sustenance for their faith in future ages. These three classes of matter seem to cover all that we find in the Old Testament; and a similar general grouping might serve also for the books in the New Testament. They also consist of narrative, and of teaching, comment, and inference more or less closely related to the narrative; and all of it such as is permanently needed to inform and sustain his people's faith and work.

This view implies a fairly comprehensive control and even overruling by God's providence of the scriptural books, both in respect of their contents and of their collection and acceptance as scripture. We have already argued that one thing it does not imply is exact factual inerrancy; another thing we may easily infer from an examination of the text that it does not imply is that it should be completely and definitively intelligible to any one who studies it with good will, intelligence, and prayer. On the contrary, what God teaches his children through it varies as their characters and abilities vary, and as the occasions vary in which this or that lesson is needed. There are certainly better and worse principles of biblical interpretation in a general way; but it is also true that God teaches people out of the scriptures in any amount of different ways, including ways which do not appear very sound if given abstract formulation. There is no reason to doubt that people to whom it has seemed reverent to seek God's will through *sortes biblicae* have been taught by him in that way; and so have others by methods which to any reader of this book would be obscurantist and unintelligent. But this is of course no argument against taking trouble to understand and use methods intrinsically better.

Principles of biblical interpretation will be discussed in a later part of this chapter; and before that, some attempt will be made to estimate the interlacing contributions of the biblical text and of the Church's tradition to our assimilation of what God has to teach us about himself. A proper balance between these two mediators to us of God's authority would almost solve the whole question this book is written to discuss; or, to put the same thing otherwise, a main object of our discussion is to help towards a right balance between the authority of the biblical text and the authority of the Church's tradition in the forming and informing of the Christian's knowledge of God and of God's will for his service in mind, heart and will. The Bible is not at all like a fire-fighting manual or a drill book, whose meaning and application is meant to be definitive and as foolproof as possible; it is a medium of teaching of an altogether different kind. Whether and what we learn from it depends very largely on the context in which we read and study it; and among the chief features of a fruitful context is loyal and active sharing in the Church's life and work in all parts of it: worship, belief, morals, witness, service, and everything else in which we can share. It was suggested in Chapter Two of this book that authority in belief ought not to be isolated from authority in all the other features in the life of the Church, and that if it is isolated, something goes wrong. The Bible and the Church's living tradition interlace and support each other in informing and sustaining the Christian's participation in all parts of the life to which he is dedicated as God's adopted child and servant in the Christian family. But where everything interlocks like this with everything else, it is certainly difficult to make clear statements about what the Bible itself contributes.

INSPIRATION

The reader may have expected that great use would be made in this discussion of the word inspiration, but in fact it does not seem to be of much value in explaining anything that any reader of this book is not clear about already. No doubt it implies that God helped the human writers of the Bible to see and express what he wanted them to see and express, so as to contribute to a body of literature which was to fulfil the function of scripture; but so much, presumably, all Christians who are at all orthodox are certain to assume, and a discussion of this concept of divine inspiration is not likely to take them much farther.

The concept as traditionally held and used has most commonly been applied directly to the words of scripture, rather than to the writers of it, though in modern times there has been something of a swing the other way. 'Inspired' literature has sometimes meant the Bible as opposed to all other literature which is 'uninspired,' and both words have appeared in this sense in the titles of books. Sometimes God has been thought of as having dictated the words of scripture to the human writers; thus Pope Leo XIII, in his encyclical *Providentissimus Deus* of November 1893, says 'All and the whole books, which the Church receives as sacred and canonical, with all their parts, were written at the dictation of the Holy Spirit' (*Spiritu Sancto dictante;* Denzinger, 1951). It is true, and often pointed out, that the word 'dictare' in Latin is not quite so restricted in meaning as 'dictate' is in English; but the difference is not great. It has

sometimes been supposed that the minds of the human writers
were wholly superseded by the divine author while they wrote
scripture. Or else a distinction has been made between the
linguistic and stylistic habits of the writers, which were un-
affected, and God's complete control of these for the composition
of inerrant matter. It is too easy to meet such statements as these
with cheap derision : the problem is a real one, and remains in
the last resort inexplicable. Has God in fact guided a number of
human writers at widely different dates, so that certain of their
writings, when collected, should form a permanent means by
which he would inform and sustain his people's faith? Any idea
of what scripture is which is tolerable to an orthodox Christian
must answer yes to this question. We may demur to the use of
such notions as divine dictation, or supersession of some or all
the human writers' faculties; but we shall certainly have to posit
miraculous overruling in some sense.

Perhaps we shall be inclined to see the miracle most conspicuously in the processes of growth, selection, and canonization
of the books, in the inclusion of this and the exclusion of that.
Even so, a large number of human writers were in fact enabled
by God to compose what would, through however long a process of combing out, collection, and tradition, form permanent
scripture for the Church of God. The reason why we are likely
to be shy of such notions as dictation and supersession of human
faculties is that we believe that in this matter, as in others, God
does not in fact work like that. We seem always to have his
'treasure in earthen vessels' : prayer is not a mechanical or auto-
matic device for converse with God; the sacraments are not like
that either; the Holy Spirit teaches and guides us, not usually by
unambiguous and definitive formulae, but on condition of our
patient and careful waiting, scrutiny, and readiness to seek and
discern human advice. It is by the analogy of these other gifts
that we shall be inclined to estimate the gift of Holy Scripture.

The use of the term inspiration to describe the impact of God
on the human writers of scripture is wholly acceptable, but does
not explain or assert anything beyond what all orthodox Christians assume. We shall also wish to say, not that other literature
is simply uninspired, but that God has in some degree taught and
guided the writers of scripture in a distinctive way, in view of the

distinctive purpose for which scripture was to be written. Other writers are taught and guided by the same Holy Spirit of truth, and for this teaching and guidance the word inspiration is also appropriate; for God certainly uses other writings besides scripture to promote his truth and make known his will, but in ways different from the way he uses scripture, precisely as scripture has a purpose in his providence which no other writings share. All this is true, but it is also truistic.

A Greek adjective meaning 'inspired by God' occurs once in scripture, at 2 Timothy 3 : 16, though it is not quite clear whether the meaning is 'all scripture is inspired by God' or 'all scripture inspired by God is . . . ' In any case we do not know how the author of this epistle thought of the inspiration of scripture; he may well have been as un-Jewish in this respect as in many others, and in any case, as we have seen, it is extremely unlikely that any Christian in New Testament times simply took over the current Jewish view, since a main Christian task was to keep saying that the Jews had misinterpreted scripture fundamentally.

For these reasons it will be better to make no further use of the term inspiration in this discussion, though some of the meaning it expresses will often be relevant.

BIBLE AND CHURCH : AUTHORITY NOW

The authority of the Bible is a vast subject, which in its full meaning is the whole concern of this chapter. What is intended now is to make a few guiding statements in a provisional way, with the argument of the preceding chapters in view, especially of Chapters Two and Three.

The authority of the Bible is not isolable at all : it is always correlative with the authority of the Church, and to some extent also with that of the individual's conscience as it is guided by the Holy Spirit; and the relation between these authorities, though hard to express neatly in words, is not hard to understand, though there are those who advise a marked subordination of Bible to Church, and others who advise the converse.

Enthusiasts for the work of the Bible Societies sometimes tell us that the distribution of copies of the printed scriptures is by itself of great value; that the reading of the Bible, even apart from the context of any Church life, leads people to Christian

faith and to the practice of prayer; and that the Bible by itself
will direct people to the Church, so that they are disposed to seek
baptism and faithful membership in it, even without their being
led that way by any other agency.

No doubt cases are known in which this has happened; but it
is not at all likely to do so in isolation from the work and witness
of the Christian Church, or at least of missionaries sent by the
Church. It is far more likely that the Bible, read out of the context of the Church, will at least bewilder and confuse; it may
well do worse than that, and breed heresies or even new sects. It
is not to be supposed, of course, that the whole crop of heretical
sects which began somewhere in America during the nineteenth
century had their origin simply in the reading of the Bible by
ingenuous persons of unusual psychological make-up. In each
case there were other factors at work too. But many at least of
these sects propagate themselves by their own interpretations of
the Bible, on the assumption that the Church has interpreted it
wrongly, and that there is no reason why any one should not draw
some new meaning out of it, in no positive relation to what it
has been taken to mean by Christians, however uninterruptedly
and unanimously.

This is not the place to discuss Mormonism, Adventism, or the
so-called Jehovah's Witnesses; but there is no doubt that their
reasoned basis, especially that of Adventism, consists in a sincere
study of the Bible, uncontrolled by the tradition of the historic
Church. And we may meet individuals who have evolved for
themselves the most extraordinary systems of belief by the same
procedure; such cases are well known to parish priests who
attempt general visiting within their cures. The present writer
remembers coming across a polytheist who claimed to have got
his belief from the Bible : the Old Testament, he said, had many
different names for God, which plainly could not all refer to the
same God; and the New Testament said in so many words 'there
are gods many, and Lords many' (1 Cor. 8 : 5). The context of
this last text he cared nothing at all about.

A number of true arguments are familiar to us in favour of
subordinating the authority of the Bible to the authority of the
Church, and a number for the converse procedure. For the
former view it is said that the Bible is a history of the Church :

of the Jewish Church from Abraham onwards, and of the Christian Church from its beginning until the close of the Apostolic age. The canon of scripture was formed by the Church as guided by the Holy Spirit; it was in no way forced on the Church, or given to the Church ready made. All the books of scripture were written by members of the Church, talk the Church's language, assume the Church's beliefs rather than attempt to prove them, and were never expected to make sense or be convincing outside the context of the Church's life. Further, at every period since its canon was formed, scripture has been disastrously misinterpreted when read independently of the normal belief and practice of the Church. The inference may then be drawn that scripture is an instrument subordinate to the Church; and sometimes that, at any rate in theory, the Church might add to or subtract from the canon. On this view it would never be possible to appeal to scripture for the reform of the Church's current faith, morals, or practice.

On the other side it is said that the Bible is the word of God to men; though it was written by churchmen and recognized by the Church, it was as much a gift of God *to* the Church as the sacraments are. This parallel is certainly not a perfect one, but it holds in many respects: the Church did not invent the sacraments, or give them their authority or efficacy. They are given to the Church by our Lord's appointment; yet it is for the Church to administer them and to maintain them at all times. The Holy Spirit 'blows where he wills,' and may at any time deal with people apart from sacraments or scripture. Yet the special gift is in each case a treasure committed by God to his Church for obedient and reverent use; the Church is neither its maker nor its master, and may not alter it, dispense with it, or treat it as optional.

Perhaps the positive functions of the Church in relation to scripture, and of scripture in relation to the Church might be summarily stated in this way: the Church must reverently keep, study, and seek God's word to it in scripture. The Church has access to its meaning and implications, as no outsider ever has, since it is addressed to those who are living as members of God's Church, and to no one else, except incidentally. There is a real truth in the modern saying that the Church must continually submit itself to the scripture as standard and judge of its health, though this truth is commonly wrapped up in such uncouth jargon that it is hard to accept. Scripture remains the permanent witness to what the Gospel is, to the nature of authority under it (St. Mark 10 : 42–5), and to what the Church itself is and exists to be and do. Therefore all efforts for reform which have come from within the Church have always, and have rightly, appealed to the Bible as evidence that reform was due, and as evidence of the norm to which the Church should be restored.

This means that neither Bible nor Church is subordinate to the other; each is authoritative in relation to the other : the Church to the Bible as its guardian, interpreter, and addressee; the Bible to the Church as the revealed standard to which its life must conform or be reformed.

It may well be that at this point we detect an artificiality in the argument : something seems to be missing. There is certainly a gap if we allow only for God as controller and inspirer, and a number of human writers as controlled and inspired in compos-ing the contents of scripture. The factor which has been omitted seems to be this : that the Bible is not only the product of the Spirit who inspires and the writers who are inspired; it is also the testimony of the Church of God to the world in which it is set, and to which it delivers its witness.[1] Each book of scripture, even when it was written, was a product of the faith of the Church which included the writer and those for whom he wrote. Still more, the books as they were accepted by the Church as canonical scripture were thereby understood as witnessing to what God had taught his Church.

This is true of both Testaments equally, though in the Old Testament the books came out of a widely-spaced series of changing situations, and witness to the Church's faith at widely differing stages; whereas the books of the New Testament were all written in the situation which followed Pentecost, and pre-ceded any general popular acceptance of the Gospel by any of the nations among which their writers lived and worked. In some respects the later books show a situation changed from the one

[1] This point is well expressed in a review of J. K. S. Reid's *The Authority of Scripture* by James Barr in the *Scottish Journal of Theology* for March, 1958.

which the earlier books show; but the whole period covered by
their composition is less than a hundred years.

In any case, it is equally true in both Testaments that what is
recorded is not only the impact of God's Spirit on this and that
writer; it is also a precipitate of that faith to which God's people
had been corporately led by his guidance: in the New Testament, quite specifically by the promised work of the Holy Spirit
in interpreting to the Christian Church the things done through
Christ. The recognition of this fact does not enable any useful
sharp distinctions to be made; but a failure to recognize it does
contribute to narrowing our thinking about scripture to a concern with the respective functions of God's Spirit and of a series
of individual human writers in the production of a body of
literature. The recognition also helps us to understand why the
authority of scripture and of the Church are so closely inter-
twined with each other, and in fact inseparable.

RELEVANT QUESTIONS

Two things remain to be done in this chapter: the first is to
gather together some of the questions with which we are concerned in estimating the authoritative character of the words of
scripture, and the second is to express some positive principles of
biblical interpretation which if observed will keep us more or
less on the right lines.

On the modern literalist view of scripture, the Bible has an
independent status as a self-contained verbal expression of the
words of God; any idea of imperfection of any kind is excluded
a priori, and presumably even criticism of the literary quality of
any part of scripture is plain blasphemy, though for some reason
this point is not usually mentioned. The only remaining tasks are
(a) to fix exactly the original Hebrew and Greek text, and get a
perfect translation of it in whatever language we understand;
(b) to study this text with prayer that the Holy Spirit will teach
us what it means to us now, so that it will fructify in our lives.
In this second process we shall allow that there is something to
be gained by finding out what great Christians in the past have
found in the Bible.

It soon becomes clear that this simple account will not do,
since it ignores difficulties and complications at every point. The

first of the tasks it proposes is impossible : we cannot fix exactly the original Hebrew or Greek text, and nothing less than an *exact* text will do; and no translation of a Hebrew or Greek text can be perfect, owing to the differences in semantics and in idiom between the languages. Other considerations which have been ignored include at least the following : (a) the notion of verbal inerrancy, if applicable at all, is applicable in very different senses to the different kinds of literature which the Bible contains. It cannot mean the same thing when asserted of the Psalms, or Job, or the Song of Songs, as it does when it is asserted of historical narrative; and even the parts which are historical narrative are never just baldly that and no more. If all that is meant by asserting inerrancy is that all parts of the Bible contain what God meant them to contain, and that it could not be improved for its purpose by alteration, subtraction, or addition, the belief is quite acceptable, but inerrancy is the wrong word to describe it.

(b) How, on the literalist theory, are we to deal with such recorded actions and arguments as are not explicitly either approved or disapproved; for instance, Balaam's oracles? Plainly such things have to be estimated with regard to their context; but how wide a context? It seems that literalists often find great difficulty in regarding the context of the texts they quote as if simply given us for general application. No doubt J. H. Newman's application of St. John 13 : 27, 'That thou doest, do quickly' in Chapter XX of his novel *Loss and Gain* is an extreme case; he uses this text as illustrating the rapid recitation of words in the Canon of the Roman mass. But it is not very different from the sort of thing modern literalists often commit themselves to.

(c) What allowance is to be made for the supersession of earlier arrangements by later ones within the Old Testament? A simple instance is the discrepancy between the Lord's command to kill seven sons of Saul by way of wiping off the guilt which had caused a famine (2 Samuel 21), and the command 'the son shall not suffer for the iniquity of the father' (Ezekiel 18 : 20, and similarly at Deuteronomy 24 : 16 which is quoted at 2 Kings 14 : 6). On any other view of the character of the Bible, such things cause no difficulty at all.

Even within the New Testament, we need to ask what allowance is to be made for the topical aim of much that is in the Epistles, as for instance, in regard to what St. Paul says about women's head-coverings in church, or about conscientious scruples about the past of one's butcher's meat. In any case no theory about the words of scripture can dispense us from the need to face, or to accept the most convincing opinion of others who have faced, all kinds of difficulties which need historical and literary investigation.

(d) Most important of all, it is altogether impossible to interpret a large part of the Bible without the use of particular categories and assumptions, many of which are disputable. If we think that we are simply taking the 'plain meaning' without using any disputable assumptions, we are deceiving ourselves, and are in fact using uncriticized and probably unrecognized categories and assumptions; that is to say, those of our own time and education, which will be in large part quite wrong for interpreting scripture. It would not even solve this difficulty if we could find out all the unexpressed assumptions made by the original writers of scripture, a task which is quite impossible to carry out fully. For we need to hear God speaking to us in our situation now, not only to hear what he said to people in biblical times. This question of principles of interpretation will be the topic of the next section of this chapter; at least we can see that it involves such difficulties as make it impossible to solve them in any simple way.

A false dilemma is perhaps supposed to face us: we are told that we must either simply accept uncritically the most literal meaning which can be put upon the text, and use studies only in order to reach this kind of meaning, or else we are bound to the unacceptable policy of simply extracting such bits of the text as happen to appeal to us, and applying them according to our notion of what edifies us now. It may be that both these two policies have been adopted or approximated to at some time or other by Christians in modern times, but neither is satisfactory. The first will not do, because the 'literal meaning,' in anything like the modern sense of the phrase, is what the writers by no means consistently intended to convey, except in their baldest historical statements, and perhaps not wholly so even there. And anyhow, statements of that kind are often inconsistent with each other within scripture.

The second, or anthological, treatment of scripture abandons the whole notion of a given and complete canon, all of which is meant by God for our use. It involves the belief that the inspiration of scripture means simply that it contains what we may find inspiring; and it is very certain that this is not what Christians have meant by it in the past. Also, scripture contains a good deal which cannot simply or easily be applied in this way, and so we are left with a sort of bran-tub view: we can search for and pull out little spiritual bons-bons from an inert mass. Such a way of regarding scripture will not appeal to any one who believes that God controlled and guided all the contents of the canon.

After all this more or less negative criticism, it is time to attempt a more positive statement, at least in general outline, of the relation between the kinds of matter the Bible contains and the purpose for which it has been given to us by God.

This general purpose is to lead us to a personal knowledge of himself: not just to know what any ruler of the world must be, but the highly individual character of him who is in fact God, who has a Name, and has acted in highly specific ways for our training and salvation. He teaches us through the Bible to know him in the record of the main series of such actions, which show a distinctive and continuous scheme, whose most obvious feature is the principle of election by stages: from an individual, Abraham, to a family, from a family to a nation, and from a nation to a Church.

To this purpose the whole contents of the Bible contribute; and it is not very difficult to see how the various kinds of books in the Old Testament do contribute. Plainly, *history* is necessary; but not some objective detached kind of history. What we need and get is history as it remained in the memory of the people to whom the revelation was given; for it is the impact and the effects of the events which we specially need to know. For the same reason we need an account of the faith of the people: of what messages they understood God to have conveyed to them, in what context and through what spokesmen he addressed them, and what reactions the messages produced in them. This is just what large parts of the Old Testament are recording; and, for this purpose, legend is as valuable as fact.

Besides all this narrative matter, mediated as it is through the tradition and memory of the people, there are two other kinds of literature which plainly forward the purpose of scripture: first, collections of the messages which God gave his people through particular individual spokesmen, sometimes continued by later messages which cohere with the original collection, as in the case of Isaiah. This is the function of the books of the prophets. Secondly, we need a record of the people's faith as it is expressed in their poetry: primarily in their corporate and liturgical poetry (e.g. the Psalms and the Proverbs), but also in rather more individual writings (e.g. Job and Lamentations).

This summary account assumes that God's revelation by scripture is mediated to us, just as his original revelation to his people was, through the people's life, history, faith, and failings, rather than through the studies of separate sages and scholars. This seems to be in fact how he has worked; and it is much the same with the books of the New Testament, and indeed with his way of working through his Catholic Church ever since.

The books of the New Testament are to a great extent determined by the infant Church, whose faith and witness they describe. The first three Gospels are three individuals' formulations of the Church's corporate message, as St. Luke says in his preface. He says he wrote 'that you may know the truth concerning the things of which you have been informed' in the Church's teaching. The Acts of the Apostles is similarly very much an account of the Church's public teaching, and of its missionary policy along one very important line, namely the extension of the Gospel from Jerusalem to Rome. The First Epistle of Peter is also very much the Church's book, though no doubt issued by an individual.

St. Paul's epistles have indeed a highly individual author, but their contents deal with the Church's public concerns; and St. John writes very much as the *doyen* of the Church in a specific region. This is less true of the Epistle to the Hebrews, which has a more restricted audience in view; but on the whole it is fair to say that the books of the New Testament, almost as much as those of the Old, reflect the life, character, and faith of the Church, rather than the minds of separate sages or scholars.

This fact perhaps makes it easier for us to accept the fallible element in the Bible. Just as God entrusted his eternal Gospel to an imperfect Church for teaching and spreading it, and his grace for administering the sacraments of it, so he entrusted his word in scripture to a set of documents written by fallible men. God did not bestow impeccability or omniscience on any rulers of his Church, nor infallibility on the writers of scripture. In each case we see that this is the way he chose to work with us, and he has no further set of agents without these limitations. He has in fact consistently committed his treasure to imperfect trustees, both in his holy Church which is the Body of Christ, and in holy scripture which is his recorded word to mankind.

It is possible that parts of this discussion may have given the impression that a lifetime of scholarship is needed for the Bible to yield us more than fragments of its meaning. That is by no means the case : God teaches all his people through such knowledge as they have had access to. But it seems fair to say that we ought to make up our minds what amount of study we should undertake about biblical history, current literary forms, and so on, and then trust the Holy Spirit to interpret the Bible to us, and to teach us what he wants us to learn through it. It is certainly not the duty of scholars to keep pointing out how much there is that the layman does not know; but perhaps the layman on his side may recognize that the Holy Spirit is teaching him truth in spite of his not knowing much that is relevant. If he does not, he will be frequently disconcerted by difficulties of which he is vaguely aware, but cannot see why they remain to perplex him.

We can be sure that God does not mean us to be bewildered by the enormous amount there is to learn about scripture, as well as from it. But we can be almost as sure that he is laying it on us as a duty to find out how much trouble and study we ought to give to the subject. There is more than one legitimate sense to be given to St. Paul's remark about the scriptures having been 'written for our learning.' At least we can soon be freed from the impoverishing limitation which comes with supposing that 'the plain meaning' is assimilable without any special thought or trouble. We may often fail to distinguish between simplicity and laziness, in ourselves as well as in others; but we can be sure God

will not speak to the lazy as he will to the simple with the same
amount of biblical study.

SOME PRINCIPLES OF INTERPRETATION

It is unlikely that any reader of this book will be one who can
excuse himself from serious thought about biblical interpretation
on the plea of an educational incapacity for such thought,
though there are depths and complications in the subject which
go beyond the point to which most of us are called to penetrate.
In discussing the subject, we can draw our line somewhere near
where we suppose most readers will have to draw it.

Interpretation of scripture is a special case of the study known
as hermeneutics, which is described by the great German philo-
sopher who dealt with human studies, Wilhelm Dilthey, as 'the
technique of the exegesis of written records.' This would normally mean finding all that the writer meant to say, and some of
the methods involved would be the study of the writer's cultural
environment, of his personal idiosyncrasy, of his unexpressed
assumptions, of his estimate of his readers' limitations, and other
things of the kind. But scripture is most plainly a special case,
for here we have not only to interpret the writers' minds and
assumptions, but also through them to try to see why the texts
they wrote have a place in the canon. It would be too ambitious
to say we need in our scriptural hermeneutics to find out what
God meant by the written matter; but ultimately that is the
direction of our aim, and it goes beyond what is required in the
interpretation of other literature, or at least its place there is not
usually considered.

It is plain that the difficulty of interpreting texts varies
enormously according to the kind of text one is concerned with.
Thus, there is hardly a hermeneutic task at all with such a text
as 'Please keep off the grass'; thought of a kind is needed, but
hardly any discrimination or tact, with such texts as railway
time-tables or telephone directories. With a play of Shakespeare,
or with great lyric poetry, the hermeneutic task calls for all the
resources we can bring to it, and we know very well that we
cannot discharge it adequately or definitively.

The task of interpreting the Bible varies a great deal in
different parts of its text; it is at its simplest, perhaps, with the

H

genealogies and lists of names such as occupy most of the first four chapters of Numbers or the first nine of 1 Chronicles. But even here a hermeneutic task exists. We ought to attempt to see why the writer put the lists in his book at the place and at the length he did put them there; why he began and ended them where he did, and grouped the names as he did. It is not very hard to form some idea of the scope of the task demanded by the other kinds of writing of which scripture consists; what is much harder to see, and is in fact highly controversial, is to decide what methods of interpretation are legitimate and fruitful, and how far they are so, and to decide which of them are applicable to this or that part of scripture, and in what order of priority.

This subject is in fact one of such vast difficulty and complication that no more can be attempted in the few pages available for it than to make a few general remarks, most of which will suggest further argument rather than present any conclusions. It will be taken for granted, and not further mentioned, that certain spiritual qualifications are always relevant: the genuineness of the interpreter's Christian faith, the consecration to God of his mental and other powers, and his practice of studying the Bible after prayer and with request for the guidance of the Holy Spirit.

Some attempt must no doubt be made to understand and to enter into the interests and assumptions of the original writers. But this task is never completely feasible, and even if it were it is not sufficient. We need to know not only what the author meant, but also what God means to say to us now through his writings. There is then a task on hand which is much less prominent when we are interpreting secular literature, though all the principles we need in doing that are needed also in interpreting scripture. It is no good saying that we can go straight to the Bible, and it will interpret itself. No book can possibly be its own interpreter in any important sense. The sixteenth-century reformers were apt to say the Bible was self-interpreting, but it is easy now to see that Luther, for instance, undervalued the Epistle of James, the Epistle to the Hebrews, and the Revelation of St. John.

For any fruitful study of the Bible, we have to apply some

principles of interpretation to it, which derive partly from the ways in which we actually think; and so far the risks of subjectivity are necessary risks. And, more than this, unless we come to the Bible with our own real concerns, it remains unfruitful for us; and it is always *we* who are interpreting it. You cannot by-pass this by saying that the Holy Spirit is the interpreter, for the Holy Spirit is not to be harnessed in any such way, for our convenience. The intellectual modern literalist may think he is interpreting scripture without using any extraneous principles. But in fact he is necessarily giving some place to the doctrinal, denominational, and many other assumptions usual in his own environment; and he is handicapped by not recognizing that he is doing this.

The writer of this book recognizes clearly what every chapter of it no doubt plainly shows, that he interprets scripture on the assumption that it is the Church's book, and therefore is in accordance with the faith and morals which the Church holds and teaches. He believes that without this assumption he would misinterpret it, and that this is the main reason why those who do not accept the Church's faith and morals do in fact misinterpret it. This procedure is not viciously circular: we do not believe the Church's teaching to be true *only* on scriptural grounds, or believe in the Bible *only* because the Church commends it to us. But perhaps enough has already been said in this chapter about the relation to each other of the Bible and the Church.

It remains, no doubt, important to be as clearly conscious and as sanely critical as we can about the presuppositions with which we interpret scripture; and if we are efficient in this, we have as much objectivity as is attainable by any one who believes that the Bible is important for his own life now. Plainly, the kind of detached objectivity which an unconcerned, uncommitted, and disinterested student might boast of is quite futile and sterile in dealing with a literature which, if it is worth serious effort, is so because it carries continual existential implications for its readers. It is always the personal interest and involvement of the reader that must give the text its focus and perspective; and this fact sets a selective process in motion, involving value-judgments of all kinds at every step. It is thus no use at all to lament the risk of subjectivity, and if we trust the guidance of the Holy Spirit we shall be under no temptation to lament it. We cannot exclude philosophical and other principles which are extraneous to the Bible itself; and for this reason we should be chary of blaming modern writers who may use some principles of this kind which make no appeal to ourselves, unless they use them uncritically.

The general hermeneutic method which is to be applied to scripture as well as to any other literature is usually called the historical-critical method. Whenever this is said, the literalist is apt to take alarm; and he is right in calling for caution against applying it to scripture in *exactly the same way* as to other literature. For in important respects scripture is a special case. Since it is God's word, we can assume that it contains nothing superfluous or unworthy of God's purpose in giving it to us; but it is very easy to be over-confident in deciding what is or is not superfluous or unworthy, and it seems to us now that many liberal theologians of the last hundred years or so were a great deal too ready with objections to this or that part of scripture on this ground. Still, with this proviso, the historical-critical method is the same method for any literature.

The text is to be evaluated by using all available relevant information to relate it to historical events, and to the culture and beliefs prevalent in the circles in which each part of the literature was produced. That is why the critics spend so much effort in dating every part of scripture; until they have done that as well as possible, the meaning cannot be properly understood. Indeed, there is often more than one relevant date to be fixed, for pieces of earlier writing were often incorporated in later compilations, as for instance in the Pentateuch. It may be that the analytic zeal of critics has sometimes caused them to be unconvincingly minute in this part of their task; but the task itself is a necessary preliminary to any further evaluation of the literary content.

This whole task, in all its stages, is commonly known by the name 'higher criticism,' to which the opponents of all such serious study of scripture have somehow succeeded in affixing a sinister implication. But this is quite unfair: the phrase simply means the application of all relevant knowledge to the analysis of literature, so as to evaluate it historically and culturally. This is the only way to an intelligent and sympathetic understanding of it. No doubt it may be, and sometimes has been, pursued arbitrarily, irreverently, or arrogantly; if so, there has been bad and inefficient criticism, for criticism in this context simply means evaluation. The remedy is always better criticism, which does not at all imply more timid criticism. And it is fair to point out that the literalist is not refraining from higher criticism; he is performing it on different principles, and usually bringing a narrower range of knowledge to bear on his performance.

It may be that people are sometimes afraid of the task of criticism, and are tempted to shirk it, on the ground that there is often no more to be had than tentative and provisional conclusions. But the same kind of limitation must attend all our attempts to understand God's providential workings in his world. The effects of human sin and blindness are never to be ignored; and we must always try to see how, and how far, God has over-ruled them in the furtherance of his purpose. There is no reason to suppose that, if God has not by-passed the scriptural writers' human limitations and liability to error, he has not accomplished his purpose; this would be to beg the question at issue. Part of the aim of this chapter is to suggest that an inspection of the text of scripture shows that there are in fact errors in it, and also instances of imperfect apprehension on matters which are not trivial. If this is true, the conclusion is that God meant to give us a record of his saving actions which have these features; not that they ought to be denied or explained away. There is certainly something analogous to them in the means by which the other gifts of the Gospel are mediated to us under his providence; and, in the case of scripture, whatever we might expect *a priori*, the same thing seems to hold. He may well have made human liability to error, as we are told he has made man's wrath, to turn to his praise.

Scripture is in fact a particularly favourable field in which to see through the effects of human limitations; for we do know in general what its aim is in God's purpose. Still, the details of it remain an open field, calling for the application of all our resources in reverent and relevant criticism. We can easily see what this means in practice from any competent modern biblical commentary written by a committed Christian who is equipped for his work.

One kind of task which is apt to be shirked is the careful relating of text to context. First, there is the literary context, at least of the whole book in which the text is found, and often also the relation of the book to other biblical books as well. Thus, for instance, it is no good trying to interpret the first half of the book of Joshua without regard to Deuteronomy, or the Revelation of St. John without regard to the parts of the Old Testament which determine the expression of its author's visions. Secondly, there is the historical and cultural context in which the book, and often the earlier texts from which it was compiled, was composed. Thirdly, biblical interpretation requires attention to the history of interpretation in the Christian Church from the earliest patristic writers onwards. This is not a merely antiquarian procedure : it follows directly from the belief that God has given us all parts of scripture to instruct and guide his people in their knowledge of him and of his ways. If we are to be properly instructed by him through any part, we ought to know how he has instructed earlier generations of Christians through it.

The great principle of interpretation which is especially associated with Luther remains of the highest importance : that scripture is scripture because it deals with Christ. It may be that Luther sometimes undervalued those parts of scripture which he could not see did this; but if so the principle was not applied broadly enough. It will not by itself do everything, but no other principle will do as much. It follows directly from the belief that the primary function of scripture is to be the record of God's central procedure for man's and the world's salvation. What we need above all to know is the relation of anything in scripture to the climax of this procedure in the work of Christ. There is no doubt at all that fanciful connections have been imagined in this respect, but at least within the Christian family they do not do much harm. A neglect of the principle, on the other hand, can constantly do very great harm. This was a main vice, for instance, of the old-fashioned liberal habit of regarding Old Testament history as chiefly the story of human religious education, with little attention to the other respects in which it formed the preparation for the coming of God's Son in human flesh.

Two methods of interpretation have had great prominence at various times; they go by the names of allegory and typology respectively. These two are related to each other, but are by no means the same thing. Allegory interprets scripture as teaching moral or spiritual lessons which are by no means evident in a plain reading of the text. Its normal application is to narrative, and to particular details in narrative. When so applied, no denial is intended of the literal or historical sense of the narrative, but a symbolic meaning is taken as more important than the literal one, often indeed as wholly predominant over it. In extension of this method, allegory has often been used to interpret parts of scripture which are not narrative, but poetical or didactic.

The method in a rather extreme form is characteristic of the Jewish writer, Philo of Alexandria (c. 20 B.C.–A.D. 50). Though he recognizes that the characters in the Old Testament narrative are historical persons, he cares much more for spiritual or moral lessons which may be drawn from what is said of them. Thus, of Abraham's two chief wives, Hagar means general culture and Sarah means true wisdom; and the wise man (Abraham) will co-habit with both, but give more honour to the latter. In Christian patristic interpretation, allegory is especially found in such writers as Clement of Alexandria (c. A.D. 150–215) and in Origen (c. 185–254). But there is allegorical interpretation within the New Testament, though on a small scale. St. Paul says he allegorizes what is said of the same two wives of Abraham, Sarah and Hagar, and of their respective sons (Gal. 4 : 22–31). He also allegorizes the precept in Deuteronomy against muzzling a threshing ox, and applies it to the duty of supporting a Christian missionary (1 Cor. 9 : 8–10).

This method is nowadays commonly disliked, and no doubt it has often been fancifully employed by writers and preachers. But a complete rejection of it would cause very great difficulties, at least to any one who believes that nothing in scripture would have been better omitted from it. The cursing Psalms, for instance, have always been used, both in the Jewish and in the Christian Church, and must at almost all times have been taken allegorically. It is not just a modern ethical insight that one does not ask God literally to bereave one's enemies of their nearest kin, or wish his blessing on those who dash their children against the stones. For a few years about a generation ago, this rather obvious fact seems to have been commonly forgotten. Thus, in the unfortunate attempt to revise the Prayer Book in 1927–8, brackets were put round some of the most conspicuous of such passages in the Psalter, as if there were a serious danger of their being interpreted literally; though this procedure raised in an acute form the awkward question whether all previous generations who had used the whole Psalter in their devotions were either stupid or bloodthirsty. Ordinary good sense seems to have soon returned, and the large public which enjoyed C. S. Lewis' book *Reflections on the Psalms* (Bles, 1958), appreciated his comment on verse 9 of Psalm 137, 'Blessed shall he be that taketh thy children, and throweth them against the stones.' The comment contains these words (p. 136): 'I know things in the inner world which are like babies; the infantile beginnings of small indulgences, small resentments, which may one day become dipsomania or settled hatred. . . . They begin whimpering to us "I don't ask much, but," or "I had at least hoped," or "you owe yourself *some* consideration." Against all such pretty infants (the dears have such winning ways) the advice of the Psalm is the best. Knock the little bastards' brains out. And "blessed" he who can, for it's easier said than done.'

Another good instance is the Song of Songs (Canticles). It was not early or easily accepted into the Jewish canon of scripture, and when it was accepted, it can only have been as an allegory of the Lord's love to Israel his bride. Whether or not it was explicitly recognized that the book was originally a collection of secular love poems, it could certainly not have been taken as scripture except allegorically, even if not always in the full-blown way we find it so taken by, for example, Origen, St. Bernard, or J. M. Neale.

It is probably just as well that we do not nowadays resort quite so readily to allegorical interpretation as has sometimes been the fashion in the past; though it was the normal practice in mediaeval preaching to make a healthy and effective use of this method (see Charles Smyth's *The Art of Preaching*, S.P.C.K., 1940; and G. R. Owst's *Literature and Pulpit in Mediaeval England,* 1933 and 1961). It is fair to say that the common modern attitude of wholesale contempt towards all allegorical interpretation of scripture is unintelligent and impracticable. Allegory is already implied in principle when it has been recognized that biblical narratives are recorded partly in order to teach us something about faith or morals, and there can be few Christians who would not admit as much as that.

Typology is a method of biblical interpretation which, strictly speaking, is applicable only to narrative, and by extension to poetical allusions to historical events. It compares an earlier occurrence, as a type, with a later one, its antitype; and normally an Old Testament type with a New Testament antitype. The general, and perfectly sound, principle on which it rests is that God's saving plan is one consistent plan all through, and that therefore things in the pre-Christian stage of it will often correspond to things in its later and Gospel stage; and that to take notice of these correspondences is a profitable exercise for us.

Thus St. Matthew refers to God's calling his son Israel out of Egypt, to compare this with its antitype in our Lord's early childhood (St. Matt. 2 : 15); our Lord uses the type of Moses' lifting up the serpent in the wilderness for the healing of God's people (St. John 3 : 14), of the manna in the wilderness given for their sustenance (St. John 6 : 32), of the Suffering Servant in Isaiah (St. Luke 22 : 37), and of the Son of Man in Daniel (St. Mark 14 : 62). In each case he is himself the antitype. Particular persons in the Old Testament story are especially used in the New Testament as types of our Lord; for instance Adam in Rom. 5 : 12–19, 1 Cor. 15 : 22 and 45; and often by implication. So are Moses, in 1 Cor. 10 : 1–11 and often elsewhere; Joshua, whose name in Greek is Jesus; David, e.g. in St. Matt. 12 : 3 and 4; and Jonah, differently in St. Matt. 12 : 39 and 40 and in St. Luke 11 : 29 and 30.

Typological interpretation was greatly extended in the writings of the early Fathers and in Christian liturgical texts; and sometimes in a fanciful way, as with allegory. It is not easy to be confident in drawing the line between reasonable and fanciful typology, and at some periods it will tend to include less than at others. But it will be unduly timid to restrict ourselves to those instances of it which are made use of within the New Testament itself; and sometimes a little thought will show us good sense in a typological parallel which on a superficial view appears fanci-

ful. This happens, for instance, with the use in Christian liturgies
of chapter 24 of Ecclesiasticus for the festivals of our Lady. That
passage is about God's causing his Wisdom to rest on earth
among the people of Israel as its particular locus; and it is quite
reasonably applied to the human means of his Incarnation.

Typology will naturally have no appeal to any but believing
Christians, and perhaps to many of them will be mainly of use
for devotional purposes. But its principle stands quite firm at the
intellectual level: in the Old Testament, God was teaching his
people to know him through his characteristic ways of working
with them, and in his world. That was a main method by which
he prepared them to recognize his handiwork when the Gospel
should come. And in the same way the record of all this instructs
Christians now, as we have it in the two parts of the Bible.

The use of typology in Christian art at least proves that the
method has seemed fruitful, and particularly at certain periods;
for the artists were not simply expressing themselves, but intended to give profitable instruction to Christian people. We find
much of it, for instance, in the stained and painted glass of the
later Middle Ages, as in the chapel of King's College, Cambridge. We also find much of it in the Victorian glass and other
iconography of churches built under the influence of the Cambridge Camden Society and of the other ecclesiologists, who were
indeed consciously imitating mediaeval methods.

Those who find typology of a traditional kind artificial, but
yet recognize that its principle is sound, can substitute for it the
kindred method of interpreting much in the Bible by the principle of promises in the Old Testament and their fulfilments in
the New. It cannot be altogether separated from typology, but
it is simpler and less likely to run into fancifulness. This method
may almost be said to be the main one by which the Gospel was
originally preached, both in Palestine and beyond. That the
promises God had given his people in the Old Testament had
been fulfilled both in general and in detail by Jesus Christ is a
main theme of the great evangelistic speeches in the Acts of the
Apostles and in the Epistles. Emphasis on this fact has been
popularized for our generation by the work of Dr. C. H. Dodd
about the distinctive and consistent contents of the apostolic
preaching (kerygma), which first affected popular thought
through his book *The Apostolic Preaching and its Developments*

(Hodder and Stoughton, 1936, and frequent subsequent reprints).

A few typical instances of this method in the New Testament can stand for many. In the first speech of St. Peter at Pentecost it controls at least verses 16 to 33 of chapter 2 in the Acts of the Apostles; and in St. Paul's speech at Pisidian Antioch verse 23 and verses 32 to 39 of chapter 13. In the Epistles of St. Paul, reference may be made to chapter 3 of Galatians and to chapters 4 and 9 of Romans. Its use for us, both in study and in devotion, is much the same as that of typology.

A very brief summary of the main principles of biblical interpretation which have been mentioned in this section might run as follows; though not all of them are applicable on all occasions. (1) Full and bold use is to be made of the normal historical-critical method without which there can be no efficient hermeneutics at all, either of scripture or of any other literature. The writings must all be placed as well as we can place them in their chronological, cultural, and literary setting. (2) We must ask what contribution *this* passage in *this* biblical book makes to the main aim of scripture. And here the primary question is 'what is its relation to the person and work of our Lord Jesus Christ?' (3) We must make a proper adjustment between the ways we necessarily think nowadays and the ways in which the biblical writers thought. This task does not at all imply that our ways are better, but simply that there is a curtain between us and the Bible until we have made this adjustment so far as it may be needed. (4) Sometimes use may or should be made of allegorical or of typological interpretation, or of the polarity of promise and fulfilment. One or more of these three is regularly used in the choice of Old Testament lessons for Christian festivals. (5) We must never lose sight of the question 'What, if anything, will God say to me now through this part of scripture which I am studying?' This is not indeed the only relevant question, but the others are apt to be unprofitable if it is disregarded.

NOTE

In this section on principles of biblical interpretation I am very greatly indebted to an article by Prof. H. H. Rex in the Australasian *Reformed Theological Review* of February, 1960. So much so that I asked, and was kindly granted, Prof. Rex's permission to make as full use as I liked of his article. Its title is 'Hermeneutics To-day.' Prof. Rex is of course in no way to blame for the use I have made of his work. But my gratitude at least prompts this acknowledgment.

CONCLUSION

The last chapter of this book, and not the end of this one, is the place for a general assessment of the Bible in relation to the main question with which the book deals : the position of verbal matter in a Christian's faith. But a few provisional remarks may be made here, since this chapter has been a long one.

The Bible is not something isolated and prior to anything else on which our faith simply depends. Its authority is inter-related with that of the living Church which is guided by the Holy Spirit. At least part of the Bible's function is to be a witness to the Church's permanent faith, and a check to prove that this faith is in fact the same faith as was committed to the Apostles by our Lord, and elucidated for them by the Holy Spirit after the first Pentecost. Outside the Church, the Bible may guide people towards the Church ; but it certainly also guides others in very different directions. Within the Church, the Bible tests and checks belief and conduct, so long as it is taken as the Church's book, and therefore as consonant with the Church's belief, morals, worship, and work. Through the Bible, the Holy Spirit instructs each member of the Church in the meaning and implications of his relation to God, and on every occasion in the discernment of God's will.

If our faith does not simply depend on the Bible, on what does it depend? Ultimately it depends no doubt on the impact of God the Holy Spirit on us, and on nothing else. But among subordinate causes of it, none can be isolated as prior to all others. There are many causal factors, and their relative dominance varies to some extent with different Christians; and the order in which they impinge on any one is different for a child who is being brought up in a Christian family from what it is for one whom an effective demand for Christian faith meets later on in life. But the child's faith grows and deepens through much the same causes as serve to begin it in the adult convert.

Among these causes the Bible certainly has an important place, but in conjunction with other causes. Among these other causes the following usually have their place : the fact of the Church as an active body consisting of committed Christians; the life and witness of particular past and present Christians as testifying to their true source and motive; the personal influence of our family, school, and friends; our own need, increasingly felt, to recognize an ultimate ground and aim for our own life, and to see a morally and intellectually satisfying reason for the world's being as it is. As we go on in the Christian life the same factors continue to operate, and very clearly the Bible does so. So does the self-authentification of our faith in prayer and sacramental communion, and in our applying it in the particular decisions which every day calls for.

There is no special distinction to be made between the authority of the Bible and the authority of the words of which it consists. The authority of the biblical words is always conditioned by their context: within the Bible itself, by their literary and chronological context, and their relation to the whole saving work of God, of which the Bible is the record; and outside the Bible, by their relation to the life and work of the Christian Church, and to each individual Christian's life and work within the Church. Outside these contexts, the words remain almost wholly inert. In the final chapter of this book, an attempt will be made to co-ordinate the relevant factors, so that the distinctive place of the Bible within the complex can be more satisfactorily estimated.

CHAPTER VIII

CREEDS AND OTHER TEXTS

ALMOST all Christians agree that there is other verbal matter besides holy scripture which is in some sense authoritative for them; but as soon as we try to go into any detail about what this matter is, and how far this or that component of it is authoritative, we have walked right into the area of controversy. The best method in this chapter will be for its writer simply to express his own view, and to pay regard to other views only where he explicitly refers to what he takes them to be.

The general principle recommended here is that the authority of all such non-scriptural matter varies directly with its recognition as expressing the normal living faith and morals of the Church as it is extended in time and space. This principle will often fail to solve difficult questions about its application to details: for instance, it may be doubtful how universal this or that belief has been and now is; or whether what the supposedly authoritative words express is or is not really the same belief as has been held elsewhere and at other times. There is also the whole, and very difficult, question about development in Christian belief: when is a later expression of doctrine or morals a clarification of what was held, and had been expressed, before; and when is it an illegitimate extension of it, and so in this sense *new* belief?

Nevertheless, hard as it is to apply this principle, it will be taken as central in the discussion which follows here. When we apply it, we shall be bound to say that there is a scale of authoritativeness belonging to different kinds of relevant verbal matter. The catholic Creeds will come at the top; the determinations of the great Councils of the Church will come a bit lower down; lower still, the dicta of local councils and of great individual Christians; and somewhere near the bottom such pieces of oral or written advice as may be given by any one who is entitled to claim our attention to his opinion or advice. It is clear that the positing of any such descending scale raises all kinds of difficult questions : for instance, is an absolute and unqualified authority to be attributed to any of these texts, and if so to which of them? And what can an absolute authority mean, if phrases in a creed describing God's actions are supposed to possess it? Can it mean more than that no more adequate words to describe such actions are available, or ever will be available?

There is another classification of which some account needs to be taken, at least in the modern period in which the outward divisions within Christendom have been very conspicuous. A Roman Catholic will pay little regard to words which come from any source except a Roman Catholic one ; and an Anglican will at least pay special regard to Anglican pronouncements. It will be very hard to see how much complication this outwardly divided state of Christendom imports into the subject we are trying to deal with.

The general principle that the authority of verbal matter for a catholic Christian depends on the degree in which it is accepted as expressing the universal faith of the Church is no addition to what has been argued in earlier chapters of this book, but follows directly from it. Two points in particular were argued for : first, that authority in any such application of the word is the same thing as the obligation to conform ourselves with God's Church, as it has been and now is guided by the Holy Spirit. Secondly, that no sharp distinction is to be made between authority in matters of belief and authority as obliging us to accept and conform with the Church's morals, worship, work, and witness. Authority in belief is co-ordinate with authority in all other parts of the Church's life : every loyal member is obliged to accept and live by all of them.

There is a classical statement on this subject which is always quoted when it arises, and will be once more quoted here ; though in fact it says rather less than has already been said on this and on the preceding page. It occurs in the second chapter of the famous *Commonitorium* of Vincent of Lérins, a monk who wrote in the first half of the fifth century. The relevant section reads 'Further, in this Catholic Church great care is to be taken that we hold that which has been believed everywhere, always, by all. (For that is truly and strictly catholic, as the very force and meaning of the word show, which includes everything almost universally.) But this will be in fact the case if we follow universality, antiquity, consent. And we shall follow universality in this way: if we profess that one faith to be true which the whole Church throughout the world confesses; antiquity if we in no way decline from those meanings which it is clear that our holy ancestors and fathers assigned; and consent similarly, if in antiquity itself we follow the determinations and opinions of all, or at least nearly all, priests and doctors alike.'

This is valuable as a classical statement of what is a truism for any Christian who is likely to read this book; but its application in detail remains difficult, and as a rule of thumb it is of no use. For doubt about the authority of a belief is normally doubt about whether it has or has not been held 'everywhere, always, by all.' Some other limitations also seem obvious: we can hardly apply it to minor matters which may be expected to vary in different social environments, such as the obligation on women to cover their heads in church. This is no doubt enjoined by St. Paul in I Cor. 11 : 4–16; but St. Paul's point is that public worship is a very unsuitable occasion for feminist demonstrations, and when hatlessness has ceased to be such a demonstration, the precept has lost its meaning. The same kind of argument may apply to our Lord's precepts about his disciples' travelling gear when on mission (St. Mark 6 : 7–12, and parallels in St. Matthew and St. Luke). The Vincentian canon will also not be applied to questions of historical or scientific belief, though perhaps none of these can strictly be brought under the canon at all; certainly not beliefs about the shape of the earth or the relation of the sun to it.

The Vincentian canon throws no light at all on any of the very difficult questions which arise if we think about developments in doctrine and in its verbal expression. For instance, can all later expressions of doctrine which are authoritative be related to earlier ones as no more than clarifications of them? Or are they sometimes statements of what was implicit but not fully realized before? Or can we admit real developments in authoritative expression of doctrine without letting go of the admitted principle that there can be no *new* revealed doctrine? There is a clear and most informative discussion of these questions within the Church of Rome in Owen Chadwick's Birkbeck Lectures,

From Bossuet to Newman (Cambridge University Press, 1957). These and other questions about development of Christian doctrine are relevant to the subject of this chapter; but no discussion of them within the limits here available could do more than show how complicated they are, and therefore none is attempted.

In spite of these limitations, the Vincentian canon has its value as a classical statement from as early as the fifth century of what lies behind the general principle already mentioned, that the degree of authority attaching to verbal statements of Christian doctrine varies directly with its being the expression of what has been believed by the Church 'everywhere, always, by all.' This must be taken to refer only to statements of doctrine which have in some sense an official source; that is, it refers only to verbal statements which are known and classical. Plainly it has no application to some private individual's words just because they express in accurate terms what is in fact catholic belief. Perhaps an accurate account of the Vincentian principle should say that authoritative verbal expressions of belief are those which *both* express what has been believed 'everywhere, always, by all,' *and also* are classical expressions of belief which have, as formulae, been generally accepted.

A distinction is implied between the authority of scripture and the authority of such other verbal matter as is in some degree authoritative for Christians. For scripture is authoritative apart from any distinctions within it about the degree in which this or that part of it expresses what has been generally taken notice of within the Church. Other verbal matter we find to be authoritative because and so far as it is accepted as expressing belief which is catholic by the standard of the Vincentian canon. Yet in another way an advantage lies with the non-scriptural formulae; for they aim at concise and exact expression of catholic belief, whereas scripture contains little of this. All fully authoritative catholic belief is indeed *contained in* scripture: that is, the Church has rightly found it there. But by no means all catholic belief is so unambiguously stated in scripture that any external observer would be open to a charge of stupidity or disingenuousness if he failed to see it there. The degree in which important articles of catholic belief are unambiguously explicit in scripture varies greatly: for instance, the unity and almightiness of God

I

is perfectly explicit, the universal necessity of Baptism and of Holy Communion is hardly less so, and the doctrine of the Trinity at least implicit.

Still, the sense in which all standard catholic belief is 'contained in' scripture is probably impossible to state inclusively; scripture can always be quoted in support, but the probative force of the quotation varies very much. The obligation to baptize infants seems clear enough from scripture to most Christians, and makes a very fair showing by the Vincentian canon; yet it has been denied by many devout and intelligent believers since the sixteenth century. Conversely, the obligation of the Christian Sunday is not seriously disputed, though it is very far from clear from scripture alone. The question of the relation of tradition to scripture is unavoidable, and will call for some discussion presently.

But much that has already been said is highly controversial, and will certainly have raised objections in many readers' minds. 'Far too elaborate,' 'no use to any one except scholars,' 'a steep slope with no firm holds,' and 'how can any one tell where he stands?' might express the general line of these objections. And it is beyond doubt that many Christians propound clearer and neater ways of classifying the authority of verbal expressions of belief. For a Roman Catholic, the authority of such words depends on whether, and on how formally, they have been promulgated by the See of Rome. Some other orthodox Christians account as inerrant at least the words of the 'Nicene' and the Apostles' Creeds, and also the formal definitions of certain Councils of the Church, usually the first four, six, or seven of those commonly known as Oecumenical.[1] Outside these defined words, their position may not differ much from that which has been sketched in this chapter. Protestants commonly make a very clear distinction between the authority of the words of scripture and that of any other words promulgated by the Church; and some of them may attribute little more to any such words, even to the Creeds, than to regard them as valuable registrations of what most Christians believed at some particular date. In the

[1] The list is: Nicaea I, A.D. 325; Constantinople I, 381; Ephesus, 431; Chalcedon, 451; Constantinople II, 553; Constantinople III, 680; and Nicaea II, 787. No further councils are accepted as Oecumenical by the Eastern Orthodox Church, though many are by the Church of Rome.

case of formulae still in common use, they would presumably call them a venerable link with the past, or some such thing.

But if the principles argued for in earlier chapters of this book are true principles, our complicated estimate of authoritative verbal matter outside scripture is no particular disadvantage at all. For a Christian's belief does not depend on any such words, and it is well if he is not tempted to make it do so. There is a limited sense in which it may perhaps be said to depend on scripture, and the last chapter attempted to describe what these limits are. But the function of other authoritative words is to witness to what is in fact the belief of the Church, and in no way to act as its foundation. In practice, as has been argued in Chapter Two, the Christian accepts, and lives by, the normal belief of the Church for the same reason as he accepts and lives by the Church's worship, work, and all the rest of it. It was also argued that, in normal circumstances, the desire to know the exact extent to which he is committed to this or that formula is a sign of defective and not of healthy faith ; and the analogy was suggested of a husband who was apt to be concerned about exactly what obligations he committed himself to when he married his wife, and the extent to which he then committed himself to them. In special cases, the question may no doubt arise, for the Christian or for the husband ; but for both the situation is happier and healthier if it does not arise.

The subject of scripture and tradition must now, as was promised above, be considered in a little more detail. This question has for some time been a very live one among Roman Catholics, and has had an important place in their second Vatican Council, where there has been a generous desire to deal with it in such a way as not unnecessarily to alienate non-Roman Christians. It was also, as is well known, a crucial point of debate during the reformation of the sixteenth century. At that time the Council of Trent, at its fourth session (April 8th, 1546), asserted that 'The holy ecumenical and general Synod of Trent . . . perceiving that [the] truth and discipline are contained in the written books and in the unwritten traditions, which were received from Christ's own mouth by the Apostles, or from the Apostles themselves were handed down as it were manually at the dictation of the Holy Spirit and have come to us . . . receives and venerates

with equal pious affection and reverence all the books both of
the Old and New Testament, since the one God is the author of
both, and also (*nec non*) the traditions themselves, pertaining
whether to faith or to morals, as having been dictated either
orally by Christ, or by the Holy Spirit, and preserved by continual succession in the catholic Church' (Denzinger, 783).

This same teaching was reaffirmed at the first Vatican Council in its Constitution on the Catholic Faith at its third session
(April 24th, 1870), and is referred to in Pius X's anti-modernist
oath of September 1st, 1910 (Denzinger, 1787 and 2147
respectively).

The present discussion among Roman Catholics is much concerned with the question how far scripture and tradition are *two*
separate sources of revelation; or whether, and if so in what
sense, tradition may be regarded as no more than the authoritative explication of the content of scripture. The words of the
Tridentine decree certainly seem to speak of *two* sources; but it
does not become a non-Roman to press this point, since to-day
very eminent Roman theologians are arguing that the sources are
in fact not two, but in some real sense one source. This discussion,
both among Roman Catholics and elsewhere, is of great importance both for the reunion of Christendom and in itself, and has
a strong claim on our sympathy, understanding, and prayers.

Apart from official discussion, there seems to have been for
some decades at least a tendency among Roman Catholics to
refer all doctrine, so far as they can, to scripture as its source;
and this is true even with such doctrines as non-Romans cannot
find to be supported at all in scripture, as for instance, the
Immaculate Conception or the Assumption of our Lady. It has
long been recognized as bad manners to press Roman Catholics
in any discussion about the scriptural basis of such doctrines; and
this would not be the case if they felt quite free at any point to
say they were not founded on scripture at all, but simply on
tradition.

Article VI in the Anglican Thirty-Nine Articles of Religion
contains these words: 'Holy Scripture containeth all things
necessary to salvation: so that whatsoever is not read therein,
nor may be proved thereby, is not to be required of any man,
that it should be believed as an article of the faith, or be thought

requisite or necessary to salvation.' This Article in its present form dates from the final revision of 1571; but the same thing is said not very differently in the original form of 1553. In any case it is later than the fourth session of the Council of Trent. If it is legitimate to emphasize the words 'necessary to salvation' then there is no ground for saying that the Article sets a low value on tradition in doctrine; it says no more than that *essential* doctrine may not be grounded on tradition alone, without scriptural support. If this is the right interpretation of the Article, then it is easy to support its statement from the greatest and most authoritative Christian writers; as for instance St. Athanasius' statement that 'the holy and divinely inspired scriptures are sufficient of themselves to the declaration of the truth,' or St. Augustine's that he judges doctrine 'owing unhesitating assent to nothing but the canonical scriptures.'

But it certainly will not do to underestimate tradition, either for the purpose of clarifying what is not explicit in scripture, or as the source of useful and usual, if not of necessary, doctrine. There is much in Christian doctrine and practice which makes a good showing when judged by the Vincentian Canon, but is far from clear in scripture alone. Even the cardinal doctrines of the Holy Trinity and of the Two Natures, human and divine, in the incarnate Christ are implicit rather than explicit in scripture. They can rightly be seen in scripture when tradition is used as guide and interpreter; but might certainly be unrecognized if no use at all is made of tradition for this purpose. It seems to be true that those sects and individuals who have denied these or other cardinal doctrines of the Christian Church are just those who have, in general, taken the lowest view of Christian tradition, and as high a view as possible of scripture.

Two other instances may be mentioned, which in different ways raise the question of the function of tradition in relation to scripture: the practice of baptizing infants, and the observance of Sunday as distinctively the Lord's Day in each week. It seems indeed almost certain that infants were baptized in New Testament times: if the New Covenant were to be unlike the Old, in that one could not enter it for many years after birth, this unheard-of revolution would have to be proclaimed with enormous emphasis and repetition; and of this there is no trace. Still,

it is possible to deny that infant baptism rests firmly on New
Testament evidence, as the existence of Baptists shows. It is only
by reference to tradition that we can be quite certain that infants
are to be baptized; apart from tradition some doubt on the
subject is to be expected. Though the practice of the Church on
this matter before about A.D. 200 is still a topic of controversy,
there is no doubt at all about what it was from then onwards
until the beginning of sixteenth-century Anabaptism in 1525. If
any one opposed it, at least only very eccentric Christians did so.

For every one who follows the main Christian tradition, what
is not certain from scripture is fixed by tradition. Of course no
tradition would have fixed it *against* the evidence of scripture,
but then it is not to be supposed that there would ever be so
unanimous a tradition in contradiction of scripture. Many modern
Protestants no doubt deny this last statement; but in those cases
in which this seems to them to be so, either the tradition is in fact
only sporadic or partial, or else the matter is of no great importance at all, so that no unanimity about it need be expected.

The other subject mentioned is strictly not a matter of faith
at all, but it is one of such importance in Christian practice that
it is not out of place to refer to it alongside infant baptism. The
practice of keeping Sunday as the distinctive Christian holy day
in each week is most insecurely provided with evidence in scripture, and can certainly not be said to be proved by it. No more
can be established on this ground than that this day was probably so kept in New Testament times. Only one narrative in the
Gospels is relevant, St. John 20 : 26, and that says no more than
that in fact the disciples met together on the octave day of our
Lord's resurrection. Only three other passages seem to be relevant at all: Acts 20 : 7 is better evidence for Sunday as a holy
day than the other two, but it does not actually say more than
that the brethren at Troas were assembled to break bread on
that day on this occasion. Nothing is really established about the
Christian Sunday by either of the other two texts: 1 Cor. 16 : 2
says that Sunday was thought a suitable day on which to put
money by, and in Rev. 1 : 10 the writer says 'I was in the Spirit
on the Lord's Day.' We have to use writings later than the New
Testament in order to show that this phrase meant Sunday, and
not just the Day of Judgment or something else; but the phrase

in the *Didache* (chapter 14) must mean Sunday. There is a further reference to Sunday as the Christian holy day in the so-called *Epistle of Barnabas* (15 : 9), and Justin Martyr in his *First Apology* (*c.* A.D. 150) actually calls the day Sunday, and describes the eucharist as proper to that day. This is a good instance of having to use tradition to make clear what is not clear in scripture alone.

The way in which tradition is to be used on any such subject as this can be looked on as a sort of application of the Vincentian Canon. If the matter is important enough for there to be a definite tradition about it, and if this tradition is constant and invariable, then it has great authority. When the tradition satisfactorily fixes the meaning of scripture, it will be accepted by those who assent to the argument of this book, even if they privately wish it were otherwise.

The tradition about the two matters discussed above, infant baptism and Sunday, received very different treatment at the Reformation in the sixteenth century. Infant baptism was rejected by an important minority, which has successors even to-day; but the tradition about Sunday was not questioned, though it may seem surprising that no scriptural literalists used Col. 2 : 16 for the purpose. Still, though Sunday was not rejected, the mediaeval abuse of assimilating it to the Jewish Sabbath (Saturday) became much worse at this time; Sunday was actually called the Sabbath, and in some places it still is so called.

To align this discussion with the main theme of the book, it may be well to attempt some kind of summary statement about scripture and tradition. This cannot be done shortly without leaving many loose ends and openings for objections; but it is better to do it roughly than to leave the argument in the air. Principles might be rather too dignified a word for what follows, but perhaps there are implicit principles in it.

(1) Scripture remains primary and authoritative, in the sense outlined in the previous chapter; but scripture is not to be taken as simply a corpus of inerrant words, which can be interpreted in isolation, apart from context, background, and their writers' assumptions, in the sort of way we interpret statute law. The previous chapter contained an attempt to sketch the way in which

scripture is to be interpreted, and to defend this method from liability to the accusation of failing to take its exact words seriously, or of putting our personal preferences in the place of God's objective gift to us of a body of canonical literature.

In general, the meaning of scripture is to be found in its classical interpretation by the Church; and the more consistent this interpretation is, the more authoritative it is. At the same time, Christians retain the duty of understanding, so far as their abilities allow them, the fact that this interpretation really is the meaning of scripture, and of seeing for themselves how it is right, rational, and coherent. There is a hackneyed quotation from St. Basil (Moralia, Rule LXXII), 'Such hearers as have been instructed in the Scriptures should test what their teachers say, and receive what agrees with the Scriptures but reject what disagrees, and sternly decline dealings with those who persist in such teachings.'

(2) God's word in scripture still speaks freshly and *ad hoc* to a Christian who is living loyally by the Church's belief, worship, morals, and work. Often the first part of this remark is made without the qualification of the second part of it. Of course God *may* speak so to anybody at any time; but the history of recent times provides many warnings of what may happen when the qualification is entirely disregarded. New Christian and partly Christian movements have arisen in just this way; sometimes on the basis of scripture read quite apart from the context of the historical Church, and supplemented by an independent 'revelation,' for instance in the cases of Mormonism and of Christian Science; sometimes on the basis of scripture alone, read by principles of exegesis which are at variance with the tradition of Christian exegesis, as with Seventh-Day Adventism; or on scripture read in the light of an independent set of beliefs, as with Jehovah's Witnesses.

Still, however loyally the Christian reads scripture in the light of Church tradition, the focusing of this light is never a merely mechanical task. To do it profitably, he needs a good deal more than simply the words and the meaning of the formulae of the tradition; more than simply to know their rating by the Vincentian Canon. The main practical means to keeping a right balance between scripture and tradition as consentient guides of a Christian's life is simply that he conforms himself in all respects with the Church's life, and makes a balanced use in doing this of his mental, affective, and volitional powers together. To say this is no more than to say what every chapter of this book has said from one angle or another. But there are few tasks for the Christian in which it is more centrally relevant, or more likely for one reason or another to be forgotten.

(3) All reformations of the Church as it has come to be at any period proceed by an appeal to scripture; there is no other appeal by which they can be made. But this cannot be just an appeal to scripture against the Church, or even against general catholic tradition; it must always be to scripture as a reminder of the genuine tradition, as against temporary or local aberration from the general tradition. The healthiness of actual historical attempts at reformation of the Church can fairly be measured by the degree to which this has been the appeal. At the reformation in the sixteenth century, the appeal was in too large a degree, and over too large a part of the area affected, to scripture as against the tradition of most of the Christian centuries after New Testament times. In other words, too low an estimate was made of the good things which the Holy Spirit had brought forth in the Church after its earliest period. In England great respect was paid to at least most of the tradition up to a certain time, and too little to tradition after that time. The two parts of Christian belief which suffered most from this were perhaps the doctrine of the Church itself and the doctrine and practice of the eucharist. But many other parts of the Church's life were in some degree adversely affected at this time by the taking of too low a view of tradition as against what scripture was thought to imply. Perhaps nothing in our own great theologian, Richard Hooker, did more to earn him his stock epithet 'judicious' than his sane and balanced attitude about the interrelation of scripture and tradition. It remains one among the many reasons why he is worth reading.

It may be fair to judge that the defect of the Counter-Reformation in the Roman church was on the whole simply the opposite error: that too much regard was paid to later tradition, in matters of polity as well as of doctrine, and too little to its need of reformation by the norm of scripture. What was effectively reformed, and it was a great deal, was mainly a number of abuses which could be seen to be abuses by reference to the main tradition as well as they could by reference to scripture.

(4) The individual Christian proceeds more or less in this way: he knows he will come to no good by trying to bypass any part of catholic tradition, but he also knows that in many respects tradition has varied at different times and places and that through his study of scripture he may learn very much about its true balance. He will be guided by extra-scriptural formulae according to their general acceptance within the Church as authoritative; so among current formulae he will find some kind of scale, with the catholic Creeds at one end and local *ad hoc* advice at the other.

There is one further qualification that is relevant in calling classical formulae about Christian belief or practice 'current' formulae. They may be current in different ways; some formulae were made at the time of a particular controversy, accepted as satisfactory, and then more or less forgotten in the later life of the Church. They were not doubted or disputed, but also they were not frequently remembered, except when the issues which had originally produced them were in some way revived. Others remained current in a much more important way, by their continued use in the public worship of the Church. Perhaps theoretically this does not enhance the authority of this latter kind of formulae, but at least it has greatly influenced their control over the thought of the Church as a whole. Thus, in a sense, constant liturgical use of a formula may be said to enhance its authority.

It appears to many people that a fairly sharp division ought to be made between formulae which concern matters of faith and those which concern practice, and in some cases no doubt this is so. Matters of faith, so far as they can be formulated in short phrases, are permanent and timeless, in a way in which some precepts for practice are not. It has already been suggested that St. Paul's requirement that women should veil their heads in church has now lost its point. But those practical precepts which have a high rating by the Vincentian Canon usually involve also some principle of faith, or at least closely concern the life of the Church. For instance, more is involved in our deference to the practice of infant baptism than that it rates high by this Canon; it also bears plainly on the objectivity of God's action in the sacrament, and on the recognition that its recipients do not contribute anything of value or in any degree qualify themselves for baptism.

No doubt personal faith is required when it may be had; so it is too with Holy Communion. But infant Communion is the practice of the Eastern Church, as infant baptism is of East and West alike. It need not indeed be supposed that Baptists deny the objectivity of God's gift in baptism, or suppose the candidate can contribute anything of value; they may suppose that it is in fact his will that people should be able to understand something of what is going on at baptism in order to be proper recipients of it, although the sacrament itself is as much the sole gift of God as other Christians believe it to be.

Still, for Christians in the main tradition, the following words of the late Bernard Manning will probably seem to express something which is true, important, and moving: 'In baptism, the main thing is not what men do, but what God has done. It is a sign that Christ claims all men as His own and that He has redeemed them to a new way of life. That is why we baptize children. . . . The water of baptism declares that they are already entitled to all God's mercies to men in the passion of Christ. Your own baptism ought then to mean much to you. It ought to mean all the more because it happened before you knew, or could know, anything about it. Christ redeemed you on the first Good Friday without any thought or action on your part. It is right therefore that as He acted in the first instance, without waiting for any sign of faith from you, so Baptism, the sign of the benefits of His Kingdom, should come to you without waiting for any faith or desire on your part. Every time we baptize a child, we declare to the whole world in the most solemn manner that God does for us what He does without our merits and even without our knowledge. In Baptism, more plainly perhaps than anywhere else, God commends His love toward us in that *while we were yet sinners* Christ died for us' (*Why Not Abandon the Church?*, Independent Press, 1939).

So with the tradition about the observance of Sunday as the special holy day in each week: though no matter of faith is involved, yet the tradition is of importance in the life of all Christians. It would be damaging if some body of Christians began to substitute Monday or some other day.

But the case is much harder with some moral precepts or prohibitions which have a high rating on the Vincentian principle, broadly interpreted. An obvious instance is the prohibition of artificial contraception. This is not the place to discuss that question, even briefly, but there are many Christians who are by no means revolutionary or individualist who do not believe it to be foreclosed by tradition. Their arguments are not hedonist or utilitarian, but serious theological ones. Another clear instance is the tradition prohibiting usury: but that it is an instance is about all that is clear about it. Some distinctions on this subject appear to have been made mainly in order to avoid contradicting previous rulings by Church authority, and economic and financial conditions have changed so greatly that it is very hard to get anywhere by following tradition. We have modern rulings of various authority, for what they are worth; and beyond that we do what we can by prayer for an enlightened conscience.

Conversely, it may well be held that tradition has been too lenient on the subject of gambling and raffles. Many of the relevant factors have certainly changed, and tradition is not very clear or impressive on the subject. Many modern Protestants have a similar belief about the use of alcoholic drink; but here the support in tradition for a general total abstinence is very weak indeed.

It is no doubt very annoying to find such questions as these mentioned, and yet nothing helpful said about them. The aim has been simply to show that there are moral issues on which tradition certainly has something to say, and yet its rulings are of doubtful use, since it is hard to know how far changed conditions have made them inapplicable.

It would be unwise to make any attempt at presenting any kind of definitive list of non-scriptural formulae on a scale of greater or less authority according to the principles which have been discussed. But without claiming to do as much as that, we may roughly review some of the material which would have to be placed on such a scale, with at least some indication of what would be its place on it.

Right at the top, on the principles of the present argument, and probably in the view of any Christian who has managed to persist in reading this book so far, is the Creed we commonly call Nicene. More strictly, it is the Creed which was probably accepted by the Council of Constantinople in 381, and was certainly and formally adopted by the Council of Chalcedon in 451. There is no other verbal matter outside scripture whose authority is so great. Its origin was indeed predominantly Eastern: at Nicea there had been only four Western bishops, and two presbyters to represent the Pope; at Constantinople in 381 there were no Western bishops at all; at Chalcedon in 451 only four. But the Creed is unique in the universality and the fullness of its acceptance, both in Eastern and in Western Christendom.

The only qualification which need be made to this last statement is that two additions have got into the Western form of the Creed: 'God of God' is inserted after 'before all worlds' and 'and the Son' after 'proceedeth from the Father.' The former insertion is not controversial at all, but the latter is very emphatically so. It has always caused great difficulties as between East and West, and still does so. The matter is by no means trivial, as those not informed in theology sometimes suppose; it represents an important disagreement about how we are to understand the nature of God. Still, in all other respects, this Creed has the highest authority in all parts of the Church.

But it is possible to feel that this authority is qualified by difficulties which cannot be surmounted. Two of these, related to each other, may be mentioned. First, it may be said that the language and its implied concepts are 'dated,' and that we cannot think nowadays as the compilers of the Creed thought. Secondly, that guidance is needed, and that definitive guidance is not to be had, to know how far phrases in the Creed, and even which phrases in it, are to be taken as symbolic and figurative; and how far its metaphors are authoritative now.

It is said, for instance, that such a phrase as 'of one substance with the Father' is now inappropriate, since we cannot now think in terms of fourth-century philosophy; indeed, the whole notion of 'substance' has for most people become useless, or at best quite problematic. To this should be replied that we are not committed by the Creed to thinking with its concepts : hardly more so than we are committed to thinking in Greek by its being a Greek document. Genuine translation without serious loss is as possible in the one case as in the other. And, anyhow, there is very little in the Creed which can be said to imply a fourth-century way of thinking. It seems certain that if it had been written or re-written at any later period it would have come to be much more unhelpfully dated ; it is not hard to explain what was meant by saying that our Lord is 'of one substance with the Father.' It is meant that he is God in the same sense, and is the same God, as the Father is. And there is plenty of historical evidence to clarify this, for the meaning was disputed, discussed, and elaborated in the course of a long controversy for more than a generation after the Council of Nicaea in A.D. 325 which first adopted the phrase.

It may be noted that a parallel objection is often made to accepting the word Transubstantiation in eucharistic doctrine. It is suggested that nobody can properly accept it unless substance and accidents are philosophical terms in which he genuinely thinks. But, here again, it is not difficult to find out what was meant by the use of the term, and to translate this meaning into any other terms we may think in. There may be kinds of modern philosophy into which it is difficult to fit it, and if so those who hold them will find it hard to be Roman Catholics. But most people should manage the translation easily enough ; it can be done unless you dispense with all ontology whatsoever. There is, of course, always a risk of mistranslating, in this case and with the Creed ; but it can be reduced by reading and thought to small dimensions.

The other difficulty too is much less formidable than it is often said to be, largely owing to the odd idea that much of what we now take as symbolic or figurative language was in the fourth century taken as literal. This objection has sometimes been dis-ingenuously inflated by modernist Christians who wish to take other things as symbolic language which cannot at any time have been so intended ; as for instance the belief in our Lord's virginal conception or in his resurrection.

In spite of much that has been written by recently fashion-able theologians about the 'mythology' of the New Testament and classical Christian writings, and its being a hindrance to the acceptance nowadays of the faith then expressed in such terms, it seems that in fact almost everything in the Creed is expressed, and in every age must have been clearly seen to be expressed, in language which is in some degree figurative, or at least analogical. The only exceptions seem to be 'was crucified,' 'under Pontius Pilate,' and 'was buried.' Here and there in the rest of the Creed a single word occurs which *in itself* has a plain meaning, as 'Scriptures' or 'Baptism'; but there is hardly a single assertion that can ever have been taken, at least by educated people, as any more literal or self-explanatory than it is taken to be by Christians to-day.

What is no doubt meant is that the meaning intended by this language is unacceptable to those who raised the difficulty, not that the language itself involves obsolete symbols and metaphors. If a person does not believe that God's Son had any existence before Jesus Christ was born in Palestine, or that he did in fact live again after he died on the Cross, then it is not surprising that he objects to the necessarily figurative language in which these beliefs are expressed. But there is no reason at all to suppose that people were more inclined in biblical times, or in the fourth century, to suppose our Lord literally 'came down,' 'ascended,' or 'sitteth on the right hand of the Father' than we do. Probably those of little education thought so then, just as they do now; and no more then than now anybody whose education was more than elementary.

The necessary process of learning to understand what was being expressed, often in terms not congenial to us now, and of translating this meaning into words we can now use, has been going on at every period since the Bible and the Creeds were composed; every teacher and catechist does it; and there have often been, as there are now, 'modernists' who dislike the meaning and therefore object to the figurative language. They say the task of translation is impossible, when in fact the point is that they wish to jettison the content. No doubt there are real difficulties involved, and this way of stating the situation is to some extent oversimplified. Recent controversy about 'images' of God has at least made it clear to many people that the subject is complicated and difficult. The question of Christian deviationism (to borrow a political word) belongs to the next chapter, and need not be pursued now.

It will easily be seen that there is also the opposite danger, that a fear of the risks of translation may result in an obscurantist insistence on concepts and phrases which now quite fail to communicate the meaning they were once useful for. This error no doubt may cause some impediment in the Church's evangelistic work; but it is corrigible at any time, as soon as the task of translation is ventured on, whereas the repudiation of the classical language is far more likely to do harm, since it is apt to lead directly to denial of the meaning it was once, but is now no longer, well fitted to express.

It remains true and important that a classical Creed, of the highest authority, composed in the fourth century, is much less awkwardly restrictive of fresh thinking than any conceivable substitute for it would be, unless indeed it said hardly anything at all, like some new 'creeds' which have been proposed by extreme liberal theologians in recent times.

The other two Creeds, which we call the Apostles' and the Athanasian Creeds respectively, are purely Western documents, although the Eastern Church has no objection to anything contained in either of them. The Apostles' Creed is a lineal descendant of the earliest known baptismal creed of the Western Church; it had reached something like its present form by about the fourth century, but is not known exactly in its present form before the eighth. As it is our baptismal creed, and has thus been formally accepted by us or in our name at our baptism, its authority must remain very great indeed. Any defective assent to it involves, to the extent that it is defective, a repudiation of one's baptism. The proper procedure for any one who gets into intellectual difficulties about any part of this Creed, but has no inclination to repudiate his baptism or the Church to which he was then bound, is to assume, pending further light, that he has failed properly to understand the meaning of the Creed. It is probable that many intelligent and loyal Christians have been to some degree in this position, even for a large part of their lifetime. If they cannot honestly stay in this position, then it may be their duty to withdraw from the profession of Christian faith, and pray to be able to profess it again after a change of mind. If they cannot honestly pray at all, the duty of withdrawal is all the clearer.

It is perhaps a pity that the so-called Athanasian Creed is grouped as a third together with the Nicene and the Apostles' Creeds, as it is in the eighth Article of Religion. It is more of a manifesto than the other two, and does not properly conform to either of the two normal purposes of creeds : it is not a baptismal creed, nor is it the compendious statement of doctrine agreed to by a Council assembled to defend the Christian faith against topical denials of it; though it certainly is aimed partly against the heresy known as Apollinarianism. It was composed in Latin, about the end of the fourth century, perhaps by St. Ambrose.

Though it has no official status in the Eastern Church, it has found a place in some of their modern service books, and to this extent may be said to belong to the Church as a whole. But it has been much disliked by many in modern times in the English-speaking countries, and not only by those who do not believe that a right belief about God can affect one's salvation, as this Creed asserts that it does. No less a thinker than F. J. A. Hort refers, with less than his usual wisdom, to its 'substitution of geometry for life' (*Life and Letters,* Vol. II, p. 140). But, as has been pointed out, notably by Leonard Hodgson in his *The Doctrine of the Trinity,* it expresses more clearly than any other document of comparable authority the full equality in the Godhead of Father, Son, and Holy Spirit.

While the Creeds are of great authority for what they include, they are not only short and allusive, but at least one major subject of Christian belief and practice is not mentioned at all in any of them : namely, the Holy Eucharist. In the New Testament, this is something all Christians *do,* rather than a topic of doctrinal instruction; unlike baptism, which is a major topic in theology. Yet from the first it is clear that the eucharist has always been the central expression of Christian behaviour : Christians are most distinctively characterized as people who meet each week on the day of their Lord's resurrection to meet him in the way he has appointed for this life, and to look forward to meeting him as they will when he comes again as final Saviour and Judge.

It would be tedious and impracticable to attempt any comparative weighing of the other kinds of text which are in some

K

degree authoritative for all those Christians who mean by authority something like what the argument of this book suggests : the obligation to share in the Church's life and work. But it will be expected that at least some enumeration will be made of what kinds of text are in mind.

Some of the formulated results of the seven Oecumenical Councils which are regarded as authoritative both in the Eastern and in the Western Church should head our list, because they are in fact permanently built in to the life of the Church; not because particular words can be isolated and credited with inerrancy. A list of these Councils was given above in a footnote to page 130. The general point is that any one who believes in the continuous guidance of the catholic Church by the Holy Spirit will of course accept and try to assimilate the achievement of such Councils. Among their formulated results, perhaps three in particular have been most influential : (1) from the Council of Nicaea (325), the term *homoousios* (of one substance) to express our Lord's relation to God the Father; (2) from Ephesus (431) the title *Theotokos* (Mother of God) as proper for our Lady; and (3) from Chalcedon (451) an important text about our Lord's two natures as both God and Man, which has remained of great authority ever since. It has even been included in a modern reunion scheme. Each of the other four generally accepted Oecumenical Councils produced authoritative decisions which are of importance to students of theology; but they do not demand mention in this short summary. What should be said is that there is no sense in calling any particular words of a Council inerrant, but that any one who believes in the Holy Spirit's continuous guidance of the Church will for this reason accept the authority of such results of it as have shaped the Church's faith and life.

The authority of most of the other texts which are relevant to this discussion varies in some degree with the place where God has put you. To say this does not imply any relativist or pragmatic view of truth : it merely recognizes the fact that most such texts are more important for those in the same tradition as their sources, and less for others. This is not so true of the classical Fathers of the Church, whose authority will be referred to below. But it does apply to documents of local provenance. Thus Roman

Catholics know what kind of authority attaches for them to formal utterances from the See of Rome. In some of these, the defining words may be commonly held to be covered by the Decree *Pastor Aeternus* of 1870 about infallibility (see Chapter Four, above); others call for 'sincere interior assent,' or whatever it may be. But none of this can mean the same thing to any one who is not a Roman Catholic, though he should give respectful attention to Roman authoritative formulae.

If you are a Lutheran you will rightly attribute an authority to the Confession of Augsburg (1530), or if you are a Presbyterian of an English-speaking country to the Westminster Confession of 1646, which those of other traditions will not attribute. It is right that these things should vary according to where God has put you; his truth is one and invariable, but it is commended to his people according to the place where he has put them, just as in other respects too his will is made known through particular people and circumstances. If Christendom were outwardly united, the present position in this respect would alter to some extent.

This book is obviously written by an Anglican, though the fact has not been constantly obtruded. It will be expected that something will be said about the main kinds of verbal matter, apart from scripture, with which Anglicans are concerned. Plainly the Book of Common Prayer is here of special importance, not only on legal grounds, but also because it is built in to our tradition as no other extra-scriptural matter is. Even in places where some revision of the book is in authoritative use, it is still the parent book which has shaped the tradition, and not the revised version of it.

This is not meant as an argument against criticizing our liturgical inheritance, or against supporting even drastic alterations in it. But such criticisms and alterations ought to rest firmly on a loyal and humble regard for our inheritance as it actually is; and it seems true that the reformers in the sixteenth century made many serious mistakes through showing too little regard for the inheritance which they had received from earlier ages. We may hope that we shall preserve a greater regard for ours.

The Thirty-Nine Articles are not a part of the Prayer Book, though they are commonly printed at the end of it. Nowadays,

clergymen profess 'assent' to them; but no layman has been required to do even as much as this since the obligation was
removed from members of the Universities of Oxford and of
Cambridge. But the Articles have had a strong formative influence on our tradition, and cannot properly be simply written
off as obsolete. They are very plainly addressed to a sixteenth-
century situation, and this fact must in some degree affect our
attitude towards them; but they remain in fact the only standard
collection of doctrinal statements which is classical and firmly
built in to our own distinctive tradition. We are not required to
believe them to be ideally expressed or definitive in detail, but
their authority remains considerable. More is naturally made of
it by those who like their detailed emphases, and less by those
who do not.

Not much need be said about Canons for the purpose of this
discussion, but an uncertainty in the popular mind about what
Canons are is often a source of trouble, and so a brief description will be useful. Canons are not properly speaking laws; that
is, they are not an ecclesiastical kind of statute, calling for precise
verbal interpretation without regard to the circumstances of their
origin or the opinions of their framers. They are registrations of
current practice, or declarations of the mind of the Church for
the time and in the place of their production. In modern times
in the Church of England they are held to bind the clergy only;
and there is no codified collection of them since the Canons of
1604 (Canterbury) and 1606 (York), though a revision of them
is under consideration at the present. Other parts of the Anglican communion possess modern Canons, e.g., the Irish ones of
1870 and the much fuller Scottish ones of 1929. These certainly
affect the laity, whatever their formal binding force on them
may be. From these few words a sufficiently accurate estimate
may be made about the relevance of Canons to the subject of
this chapter.

The resolutions of Lambeth Conferences have no authority,
in the sense of *imperium*, at all, but they have some degree of
auctoritas: namely, such weight as attaches to the formally recorded opinions of the bishops assembled there after careful
prayer for the guidance of the Holy Spirit. As the bishops at
Lambeth are assembled from all parts of the world, and pool

their knowledge, there is much wisdom to be found in the reports of their conferences. On the other hand, there are also drawbacks, which are not always allowed for: few of the bishops are theologians, and those of them who ever have been have necessarily neglected their studies under pressure of their pastoral duty. And their assembly from so many different places is not in all respects an advantage: they come from very different backgrounds, and speak in idioms not altogether intelligible to each other; moreover, bishops are quite particularly liable to be overinfluenced by topical considerations, and where these differ greatly in the same assembly, the conditions are not very favourable to the output of wisdom. This largely accounts for the frequent vagueness and woolliness of what emerges; and another factor is doubtless that the conferences consist entirely of people who are constantly required to speak at great length on many subjects about which they are not well informed. If all this is remembered, we may be grateful for the large amount of wisdom which is in fact contained in the Report of any Lambeth Conference.

The only other texts which seem to need mention in this chapter are the writings of standard Christian authors. Among these too some are of importance for all Christians in the main tradition, and others especially for those in the writers' own particular tradition. Before the fourth century, the main important Fathers of the Church are Irenaeus and Cyprian, though there are many others with whom students are concerned, including some whose doctrinal views are partly questionable, as Origen and Tertullian. Of later times are the two sets of writers known respectively as the four Greek and the four Latin doctors, *par excellence*: the four Greek doctors are Athanasius, Basil, Gregory Nazianzen, and John Chrysostom; the four Latin ones are Ambrose, Augustine, Jerome, and Gregory the Great. None of these are always to be deferred to: all are important, though on matters of doctrine Jerome less than the others. He was a biblical scholar rather than a theological thinker.

The importance of later writers varies, much as that of official doctrinal pronouncements was said to vary, according to where God has put you. Eastern Orthodox Christians will pay great regard to, among others, John of Damascus and Gregory

Palamas; Roman Catholics to Thomas Aquinas. But none of these is to be neglected by any one who has the equipment and opportunity to attend to them.

It would be tedious to mention what writers are especially important to Lutherans besides Luther, or what to Presbyterians besides Calvin. It is well known that Anglicans make differing estimates of the great writers in our own tradition, though most would place Hooker at or near the head of their list. The aim at this point is not to do any one's work for him, but to point out that writers are relevant to us as authorities for one of two reasons : either they have influenced the whole Church for many centuries in a notable degree, or they have influenced the particular tradition within the Church in which God has placed us.

On our principles, we defer to what they say, more or less according as it has come to be built in to the life of the Church, either as a whole or where we belong in it. And in paying this deference we are well aware that these writers' authority is that of *auctoritas* and not of *imperium,* except so far as our Chapter Two was right in maintaining that one of these can hardly exist in a form which totally excludes the other.

For a formal completeness it might be mentioned in conclusion that there is a real *auctoritas,* hard to measure exactly but not to be ignored, in the written or spoken words of any one whom God has given the right to teach, warn, or advise us. And we may even in some degree confer this right on people by consulting them. In some circumstances this *auctoritas* may be of great weight; it may suffice here to mention some relationships in which the right is plainly present, without attempting in any way to assign relative weights. There is the relationship of parent to child, of schoolmaster to pupil, of confessor to penitent, of Religious Superior to subordinate, of bishop to priest under his jurisdiction, and of friend to his friend.

Our main argument suggests that no clear lines of distinction are to be drawn among all these kinds and levels of authoritative words which have been mentioned in this chapter, though their *degree* of authority varies from an almost compelling to a quite trivial one. Again, without drawing any sharp lines, we have noted that the degree of respect called for by the wording varies in the same sort of way : where the formula is a public and official one, fitted as standard for ages in the life of the Church, the actual wording has a claim on us which the wording of other texts does not have. It would not do, for instance, to produce a very good translation of the meaning of one of the Creeds, and then disregard its actual words; whereas this procedure is quite in order with, e.g., the words of St. Augustine: once you know what he means as well as you can know it, you need not mind so much about the terms in which he expresses his meaning. And this is still more plainly true of wise pieces of advice which we may receive from a modern individual.

CHAPTER IX

HERESY AND SCHISM

Since the main line of argument in this book is that authority in the Church, whether for verbal matter or for anything else, is really only another name for the obligation we have to conform ourselves to the Church's life and behaviour, some discussion is certainly called for of what in modern politics is known as 'deviationism.' The line we have taken is this: God has accepted each one of us for Christ's sake, and has joined us to himself in the Body of his Son; our whole lives, and all our activities, are to be conformed through the operation of the Holy Spirit to the life of this Holy Catholic Church. Our own wills are to be set on this aim, to live in belief as in every other respect as 'very members incorporate in the Mystical Body' of our Lord Jesus Christ. In matters of belief this means that we are to learn, understand, and assimilate the Church's belief, so far as our education and opportunities enable us to do so. It is no freedom to go in for deviations from the liberty into which Christ has freed us.

There are two classical words for deviations in our relation to the Church of God: heresy and schism. The meaning of each of these words is simple enough, but their application is difficult and complicated: heresy means denial of defined catholic belief, and schism means separation from the unity of the Church, and generally implies attaching oneself to some other body of believers in communion and allegiance. Not much thought is needed to see that distinctions of more than one kind need to be taken into account in applying either of these terms to any person or body of people.

To many wholehearted Christian people the line we have taken will be quite unacceptable: they will call it restricting or ultra-orthodox in an almost *a priori* way. We have recommended holding fast to what is normal and traditional in the Church's belief as much as to the name Christian itself, or to the basic Sacraments of Baptism and the Lord's Supper; and we have done this in each case for the same reason, that all these things are built in to the life of the Church as guided, according to our Lord's promise, by the Holy Spirit, the Paraclete.

But it is common nowadays to assume that there is no such obligation to preserve the historic belief of the Church as there is to preserve its name and its Sacraments. We have certainly not taken a line in our argument which could be expressed in the words of the old-fashioned order 'Open your mouth, shut your eyes, and swallow the lot.' What we have said is what Christians in the main tradition have always said : the revelation of God in Christ is complete, final, and once for all; it is to be understood, expounded, and applied in every age, but none of it is to be jettisoned or regarded as having become obsolete. There can be no *new* revelation, as there has been no temporary revelation ; it is all once-for-all, and to be faithfully preserved in the Church. Questions may no doubt arise about marginal matters, but these are questions about what is or is not a part of the revelation ; if anything really is a part of it, then it must be preserved.

The word tradition has for many people nowadays a fusty smell partly, but not altogether, derived from what our Lord said about the 'tradition of the elders.' It sometimes suggests a lazy unwillingness to think for oneself. The corrective to this is to find out what the Church has classically meant by the Greek word *paradosis,* which is usually, though now misleadingly, translated 'tradition.' This is admirably explained in the first of Leonard Prestige's Bampton Lectures for 1940, *Fathers and Heretics.* It is impossible here to do more than draw attention to one or two things about this classical meaning of 'tradition.' It is assumed that the contents of Christian belief are essentially *given* by God through our Lord Jesus Christ. They are authoritatively given, in the sense of committed, by him to his Apostles ; and from that time on are by the same authority *delivered* for keeping to later generations in the Church. They are not just handed on mechanically, with references to this and that text ; but the broad facts of God's saving work, and the broad meaning to be attributed to these facts, is delivered for understanding and assimilation through the promised guidance of the Holy Spirit. It is the heretics who are found insisting on the logical implications of this and that text ; the Church answers them by the broad

and coherent 'tradition' of belief, and it is to this that appeal is
made against the niggling logic of the heretics.

There are obvious reasons why this principle is now disliked :
there are so many fields of knowledge in which finality is not
looked for in the beliefs of former times. Modern discovery and
research has simply antiquated so much that was believed
before, that the notion that God's revelation through Christ is
final, and above all the notion that it cannot now be improved
or supplemented, is quite unacceptable to many. The revelation
may no doubt be in some respects better understood than it used
to be; many of its implications and possibilities of application
may be seen now as they were not seen earlier; but this cannot be
done, except very tentatively indeed, apart from the life of the
Church, and more than this is not to be expected at all.

Yet it is odd that this dislike of the Church's historic belief is
not confined to those who are uncritically impressed by the
'wonders of modern science.' It was in criticism of the con-
tributors to a very sophisticated and academic symposium published in 1962 that Dr. E. L. Mascall wrote that these con-
tributors 'seem to have lost all confidence in the tradition that
they have received, and to envisage their task simply as . . .
"beginning all over again," as if we had nothing to learn from
nineteen centuries of Christian experience.' [1] We do not find that
such people want to 'begin all over again' with the worship or
evangelistic task of the Church; but with its built-in belief this
is hardly more than their proposals amount to. It has now
become almost a title to the name of obscurantist to take seriously
the continuous guidance of the Church by the Holy Spirit in
matters of belief.

Dr. Mascall shows himself well aware of this is the passage
from which a quotation has just been made. Having said that the
symposiasts whose work he is discussing 'seem for the most part
to be more confident in the contemporary world's estimate of
the realities of the human situation than they are in the great
tradition of thought and life that they have inherited as members of the Church,' Dr. Mascall goes on 'In making this criticism, I do not wish in the least to imply that the tradition is a
rigid and finished product that can be applied to the contem-

[1] *Up and Down in Adria*, p. 11.

porary situation like an antiseptic plaster or that it is not subject from time to time to distortions and divagations. On the contrary, it is a living and growing reality whose content and possibilities we have hardly begun to discover. It may at the present time have largely lost touch with the world that surrounds it, or, perhaps we may prefer to say, the world has largely lost touch with it. But in itself, I am convinced, it holds all the resources that we need for this as for any other age, and the urgent task for the theologian to-day is first that he should live within it and do all that is within his power to penetrate into its riches, secondly that he should play whatever part he is able to play in developing its latent possibilities, and thirdly that he should, in his aspect of apologist and evangelist, do all that he can to integrate the life and thought of the contemporary world into it.'

This dislike of our inherited Christian belief is indeed in itself nothing new. At the Reformation in the sixteenth century there were many to whom it was almost an axiom that the Church had gone wrong in major matters of belief ever since New Testament times, and perhaps even before those times were ended. Ever since the sixteenth century there have been devout Protestants to whom the continuous guidance of the Church by the Holy Spirit has meant hardly anything at all. Our English Reformers rather tended to believe that things were mostly all right up to about the time of the Council of Chalcedon in 451, but after that had become increasingly unsatisfactory. Thus they claimed and valued highly the name Catholic, and readily quoted in argument such Fathers as Irenaeus, Cyprian, Basil, Hilary, and Augustine; but only very gingerly, if at all, Bernard or Thomas Aquinas.

Modern opponents of the argument from living tradition as we have used it are more inclined to assume that what the Holy Spirit taught past ages may have been all very well at the time, but is now largely irrelevant, owing partly to changes in our ways of thinking; and that he has now a new set of things to teach us. What all these people have in common is a very low estimate of the continuity and permanence of what the historic Church has been taught and has held fast to. It is impossible now to embark on a full-dress argument with their point of view : it would be too large an undertaking for a short penultimate chapter. But it is fair to be explicit about the assumptions on which our argument has been conducted, not in order to dig in to an entrenched position, but for the sake of common candour.

Within the New Testament the terms heresy and schism do not mean what they mean now. The Greek word *hairesis* means a party or school of thought, sometimes but not always with disparaging overtones to it; but the modern meaning is already approached in the latest New Testament passage containing it, 2 Peter 2 : 1. This later meaning is however perfectly clear in the letters of Ignatius (e.g. Eph. 6 : 2), and thereafter. Heresy has come to mean formal denial, whether by an individual or by a group, of the Church's defined and accepted belief. Schism (Greek *schisma*) in the New Testament simply means a division between Christian people, with the implication of self-willed uncharity. It had become a technical word in its modern sense by the time of Irenaeus, that is, before A.D. 200. Since that time, the meaning of both words has remained constant and clear, though the application of them is not simple, and fortunately the imputation of guilt is so problematic as to be virtually impossible.

What seems to have changed, at least in the popular mind, is the attitude towards heresy; and if a similar change is not so noticeable with schism, this is because the whole concept has become almost meaningless to many people. In the Prayer Book Litany we pray to be delivered from 'all false doctrine, heresy, and schism': it is unquestioned that both heresy and schism are deadly evils, which it is reasonable to mention in the same solemn petition with 'hardness of heart, and contempt of (God's) Word and Commandment.' But it is not unusual nowadays to hear someone who professes Christian faith saying in a hearty and self-satisfied tone of voice 'O course, I am a heretic,' though we should be surprised to hear him use the same tone in calling himself a murderer, an adulterer, or a blackmailer. We are not meant to infer that he regards his heresy as an unfortunate accident or unavoidable misfortune, as he might regard the loss of a leg or the death of his wife. He simply does not believe the wilful jettisoning of God's revealed truth to be a horrible thing at all. Whatever one may think of Bernard Shaw's play *St. Joan*, there is much to be learned in it from the Inquisitor's speech about heresy in Scene VI.

This changed situation at least frees us from the temptation of accusing modern heretics of the sort of self-willed pride which Shaw's inquisitor attributed to St. Joan. But it is not a healthy state of affairs when Christians no longer believe that there is revealed truth from God which it is their duty to understand and assimilate, and that the conscious neglect of this duty may imperil their salvation.

There is a traditional distinction between 'formal' and 'material' heresy: formal heresy is the wilful and knowing rejection of matters of faith; material heresy is their rejection through ignorance that they are in fact matters of faith. Strictly speaking, it is perhaps wrong to call the latter kind heresy at all, since one cannot reject what one does not know; but the terms are in current use, and it is well to remember what they mean. A similar distinction is usual in reference to sin in general: formal sin is predicated of what is both wrong and also known to be wrong; material sin of what is in fact wrong, though not known to be so.

If one is a Roman Catholic, it is clear whether one is a heretic or not: if one denies what is formally defined as matter of faith by the See of Rome, one is a heretic, and if what is not, then one is not a heretic. The only case where doubt could arise is one in which the status of a definition changes. It does not become any one who is not a Roman Catholic to say whether such a case ever actually occurs; but it certainly seems to outside observers to occur. A good instance would be the formal definition by Pope Eugenius IV about the 'matter' in the sacrament of ordination to the priesthood, to which reference was made above on page 55. It was formally defined then, but no one believes it now.

According to the principles on which this book has argued, heresy is a term applicable according to the status as a part of universal belief of what is denied; and there will also be a great difference to be made according to the pride and self-will with which it is denied. For instance, no Protestant who attaches no particular importance to any belief but what he can see for himself to be taught in scripture can possibly be more than materially heretical, even if he denies everything else in Christian belief. But of course the term heresy is not meant to have any application to

such an individualistic position as that: its use has always pre-
supposed some deference to the defined belief of the historic
Church, such as any sympathetic reader of this book will no
doubt pay.

It was said above to be fortunate that the attribution to any
individual Christian or group of Christians of the *guilt* of heresy
is impossible. Yet this fact is commonly not recognized: it is
imagined that any one who makes use of the concept of heresy
at all is involved in just this attribution of guilt, and that he very
likely rather enjoys attributing it. This is simply not the case:
there is no reason why the use of a term with such an objective
and definite meaning should involve attributing guilt or estimating culpability any more than the use of such terms as theft
or murder should do so. We can call people thieves or murderers
while recognizing that they acted under circumstances which
extenuate their guilt in any degree so that it is out of place to
blame or condemn. Law courts have to condemn or acquit, as
ecclesiastical tribunals may have to condemn or acquit of heresy;
but they are understood to do this without necessarily implying
any confident moral judgments at all.

Heresy, then, has its place in our argument as a name for the
refusal of deference to the authority of the Church in matters of
defined belief. That is to say, it is in its degree a revolt from
one's allegiance to the family and Body of Christ; and because
it is this, it must be regarded as a foul and horrible evil; as much
worse than political treason as the Church is a greater and more
important family than the State can ever be.

Schism too is a perfectly simple concept in itself: it means
separating oneself or being in separation from the Church in
allegiance and communion. But again, unless one is a Roman
Catholic, the application of the term is uncertain, and involves
questions of degree. For a Roman Catholic, any one is in schism
who is not in communion with the See of Rome; no questions
arise except concerning such states as temporary excommunica-
tion or interdict. It may be that there is little else in which all
Christians will agree on this subject except that there are in fact
at present divisions among Christians in communion and allegiance, and that these divisions are a bad thing, for the healing
of which we ought to pray to God.

It is hard for any one for whom the criterion of schism is not a closed question to resist the conclusion that there is in fact no single criterion at all, if he faces and thinks out what is implied by the evidence reviewed by Lacey in his Paddock Lectures for 1917, *Unity and Schism*. Perhaps no more can be done than to suggest *one* relevant criterion, and admit that its application still leaves many loose ends, and many important questions unanswered.

If we strike a sort of mean from the teaching of such representative men as Ignatius, Cyprian, and Augustine, it is possible to describe schism as the refusal of allegiance to one's lawful bishop; and indeed there may be no other single criterion more applicable than that. But it does nothing at all to solve the question how far schismatics are still within the Church, and how far schism necessarily implies a separation *from* it. The modern Roman Catholic phrase, sanctioned by the late Pope John XXIII, for those Christians now out of communion with Rome, is 'separated brethren' (*fratres seiuncti*), and the implications of it will differ according to which of the two words is given the main emphasis, 'separated' or 'brethren.'

Moreover, in most parts of modern Christendom it is now a question who is in fact one's lawful bishop: the criterion cannot in fact be confidently applied at all. And this is not a situation which was unusual before the sixteenth century, or even before the division of East and West which used to be dated at 1054, but is now known not to have become definitive until much later than that. The notion of 'the ancient undivided Church' now popularly held, and especially attractive to those who wish to aspire to a 'future reunited Church,' is largely an unhistorical myth.[2] There are even within the New Testament divisions which have at least partly the nature of what we call schism. The situation at Antioch described by St. Paul in Gal. 2 : 11–14 is a schismatic one, and so is the effect of Diotrephes' action recorded in the third Epistle of St. John.

At almost every period after that, schisms are recorded and admitted: Origen admits the existence of schisms when Celsus

[2] I am here much indebted to an article by Dr. H. Sasse on this subject, which he contributed to a German symposium for Prof. A. Lehman of Halle.

taunts him with them; there is Marcionism, Montanism, and
Donatism; there are the schisms between Hippolytus and
Callistus in Rome, between Pope Victor and the bishops of Asia
Minor, and between the followers of Melitius and of Paulinus in
Antioch. And so the story goes on : you have to restrict your
dates very narrowly if you are to talk of 'the ancient undivided
Church.' Schisms are in fact constantly recurrent facts throughout
the history of the Church, and most of them are far too complicated in origin and in history for it to be possible confidently
to award marks for good and bad conduct in respect of them,
either to individuals or to local churches. No doubt any historian
has his own opinions, more or less defensible, about which schisms
were specially unavoidable, and which were specially wilful and
gratuitous.

Unless we adopt the Roman Catholic criterion of communion
with Rome we can make no clear division between divisions within
and schisms from the Church ; and even then there is no plainly
satisfactory solution to the puzzles afforded by the existence of
two or three rival popes at the same time, as happened in the
period from 1378 to 1417. But we may well follow the late Pope
in calling all baptized Christians 'brethren,' and in recognizing
without imputing guilt for their separation, though we shall be
thinking of their separation not simply from communion with
Rome but from each other. And we shall never forget that this
separation concerns only earthly communion and allegiance.

Granted then that schisms exist to-day in almost every part of
the world, as they have usually existed in every earlier period in
a greater or smaller part of it, the question for the loyal Christian
is how he can behave as unschismatically as possible in the existing situation. One obvious duty is to deplore, and never in any
way to exult in, the schismatic situation; and to be penitent for
the involvement in it of himself and his own part of Christendom. He must earnestly pray for its healing. So much is probably seldom disputed, at least nowadays.

Concerning his further duty, attention may be drawn to a line
of argument in one of William Law's less-well-known writings,
*Letters to a Lady inclined to enter the Communion of the Church
of Rome*. Almost the whole of what Law says is directed exactly
to our question : granted the state of schism, how can one be as

little schismatic as the situation admits? One thing is to avoid 'taking sides' and adjudging guilt unnecessarily: if you change your religious allegiance from the one in which God's providence has placed you to some other, you are 'taking sides' and adjudging guilt in a way which you can avoid by staying where you are in allegiance. That is, a 'convert' from one communion to another is taking a heavy and unnecessary load of moral responsibility by a confident judgment about who is right and who is wrong.

Plainly this line of argument has a limited application. For one thing, it has nothing at all to say to someone who is going to become a Christian for the first time: such a person has necessarily to make a confident judgment about what allegiance to attach himself to, and cannot avoid the responsibility. It is also of no use unless one is satisfied that God's covenanted blessings are to be had where one is; it is possible for any one to be conscientiously compelled to change his religious allegiance, on the ground that his present one is impossible and untenable. But this line of thought, and indeed the whole of these letters of Law's, are well worth reading on the question of how to avoid being more schismatic than one need be in a schismatic situation.

This chapter has perhaps done little to advance our main argument, which in fact was complete before it. But it has been implied throughout that authority for the Christian is almost the same thing as the duty of a willing conformity with all our capacities to the Church in every part of its life; and therefore something had to be said about defective loyalty and conformity in belief and allegiance. Some expression was needed of the evil and horrible character of both heresy and schism, which our Litany no doubt takes for granted, but it is now common form to palliate or to deny.

CHAPTER X

CONCLUSIONS

THE general conclusion of this discussion is that authority for Christians belongs to written matter in proportion as the matter is a standing and accepted witness to the faith and life of the historic Church. The word historic has been included here because the authority of the Bible has sometimes been used in the last century or so as a supposed justification for new religious bodies, more or less Christian in profession, but in no other positive relation to the age-long Church of the Apostles and their successors. Whatever authority means in such bodies, it is not the same thing as it means for the historic Church.

Thus the *kind* of authority which belongs to written matter is secondary rather than primary, though under proper safeguards it can be appealed to directly. It is said to be secondary because the relevant texts are given to us only through the Church, and apart from being so given could not be known to have authority at all. This judgment perhaps needs some qualification in the case of scripture, since, once having been composed within and given through the Church, it remains as a standard to which the Christian can always refer; not indeed as against the Church, but as a means by which he assimilates and grows in understanding of what the Church is, professes, and does; by which also he makes certain of the legitimacy of this, and to which there is an appeal when local or particular aberrations occur or are suspected : that is, aberrations away from the Church's norm to which scripture is a witness.

Non-scriptural written matter has an authority which is in every way secondary : it depends on the Church's putting it out, and varies according as it expresses the Church's constant mind. Written matter of a local or temporary importance will plainly have more authority in its own time and place, and less as that recedes.

So far, what has been in mind is authority for those who are already Christians. What is the picture if we ask about the use of authoritative Christian written matter for those who do not profess the Christian faith? They may be given Bibles and some compendium which contains the Creeds and other matter concerning Christian life and belief. It is a bit of a gamble what will happen. They may be impressed, and inclined to get into touch with the Church; or they may be puzzled and exasperated at what seems to them a mixture of complacency and over-confident superstition. A third thing may happen: they may fall easy converts to some recent and independent body or sect which claims to have a better interpretation than the Church has. Whatever actually happens, it is unsafe to assume that written matter of authority for Christians will point others to the Church : it may do so, or it may fail to do so. Any one who wants to think further about this may find plenty of material to help him in the history and criticism of the Bible Societies. A Bible and a Prayer Book will only fulfil their proper function if the enquirer, while he studies them, is also in some personal touch with the Church itself; and even then he may be put off rather than brought nearer Christian faith.

It is not hard to think of a useful secular analogy to this situation which, though not perfectly parallel, is close enough to be worth suggesting. Suppose someone who has no inside knowledge of Scouting gets hold of a copy of *Scouting for Boys* and of *Policy, Organization, and Rules*. He will certainly be informed of much that is true and authoritative about the Scout Movement. He may be impressed and inclined to get into touch with the personnel of the Movement; or, alternatively, he may be put off by what seems to him a sort of cheap and bogus patriotism with frills borrowed from Rudyard Kipling. There is a classical and very well written statement of this kind of reaction in Harold Stovin's book *Totem: the Exploitation of Youth* (1935). A sensible judgment about Scouting could hardly be arrived at without personal contact with an actual Scout Group, or better with more than one. The Scouters would act in this case in very much the same way as Christian priests do with people on their way towards Christian faith.

If enquirers are at the same time in touch with the existing Church, then a Bible and a Prayer Book would help them very much to put themselves into the picture by familiarizing them with the Christian family's history and life, with what it does and the way it behaves. For the Bible is essentially the record of the family's origin and history : we learn there about the important people and incidents in its growth, in terms of its Lord's activity in making, moulding, and teaching it. The Prayer Book is what the family puts into the hands of its members as a guide and directory to their worship and belief. This is what is meant by saying that the authority of written matter is secondary or corollary and explanatory rather than primary.

It would be impossible to sum up our whole discussion in schematic form : definitive solutions have not been offered to any of the important questions, and such value as the discussion may have consists mainly in its raising relevant topics which call for thought. But some of the things which have been maintained may perhaps be expressed briefly in a more or less formal way as follows.

Holy Scripture has for outsiders some intrinsic authority, so far as it is genuine historical evidence of the Jewish and the Christian communities, and of their belief and practice. There is the possibility that this evidence may suggest to them the duty of conversion. Scripture has no mediated authority for outsiders, except so far as they independently respect the Church.

For insiders, scripture plainly has intrinsic authority, since it is the evidence to which the Church appeals for its history and credentials. Scripture is also the standard of reference for the correction of aberrations and abuses whenever they are found. Scripture has for insiders also mediated authority, since the Church guarantees scripture to its members ; and it is on this authority that in fact it means to us most of what it does mean.

Non-scriptural matter, such as Creeds and other definitions concerning doctrine or morals, has for outsiders intrinsic authority only so far as the formulations of it may perhaps bring intellectual conviction by themselves. It may well be that the impressiveness of Christian doctrinal formulations has often contributed towards conversions to the faith, though it may never be the sole assignable cause of them. Such matter has no mediated authority, except as reflecting the Church's.

For insiders it has intrinsic authority as direct evidence for the identity of what is now taught with what has classically been taught ; and mediated authority as it is a main way in which we learn the Church's teaching and practice.

GENERAL INDEX

BIBLICAL INDEX